AF496504

The Guide Book

Ourselves, Our Planet, Our Universe

Channelled by
TONY NEATE

Devised, edited and arranged by
MICHAEL DEAN

Gateway Books, Bath

First published in 1986
by GATEWAY BOOKS
19 Circus Place,
Bath, BA1 2PW

© 1986 The Atlanteans

Set in Optima 10 pt on 13
by Spire Print Services of Salisbury
Printed and bound in Great Britain
by W.B.C. Print of Bristol
and W. H. Ware of Clevedon

British Library Cataloguing in Publication Data
Helio Arcanophus. (Spirit)
The Guide Book:
1. Spirit writings
I. Title II. Neate, Tony III. Dean Michael
133.9'3   BF1311.H4
ISBN 0−946551−33−2
ISBN 0−946551−35−9 Pbk

Contents

Introduction

One autumn evening in 1959, after an excellent dinner in his London apartment, Robert Donaldson and I were lamenting the fact that most people — and we did not entirely exempt ourselves — seemed to be sleepwalking through life with little or no idea where we all came from, why were were here in the first place and where, if anywhere, we were going.

Bob had just spent several busy years in Harley Street, specialising in the treatment of nervous disorders, stress and migraine. Long before the word 'holistic' had been coined, Bob was treating, not isolated illnesses or dysfunctions, but the whole person: he worked on several levels simultaneously, and his spectrum of skills included diagnosis, anatomy, counselling, psychotherapy, physiotherapy, listening — a great art, little understood — humour and common sense.

The increasing stress caused by living in an intense, indeed crucial, period of our history provided the medical and allied professions with an excellent living during the 'fifties, but a philosophical streak in Bob himself enabled him to view the phenomenon in a detached and compassionate manner:

"How much simpler life would be if we all arrived here wearing a small book of instructions round our neck — which we could consult whenever a problem or challenge crops up," he mused.

I heartily agreed. We seemed, then — as the dull, ugly and rather pedestrian 'fifties drew to a close — to be living at a time when nobody really believed in anything any more. Material prosperity was proving to be something of a mirage or will-o'-the-wisp; the Cold War and the nuclear 'balance of terror' weighed heavily on us; we no longer felt that we owed allegiance to the remote and forbidding God purveyed by the Church. The young, misunderstood at home and at school alike, encouraged neither to investigate their real identity nor to develop their individuality, began to ferment.

It went two ways, as it always will. First as a destructive, vengeful restlessness that erupted into noise, defiance and extremism; and secondly, some three or four years later, came the nuclear chain reaction whose repercussions we are experiencing to this very day: a consciousness explosion, no less, embracing music and the visual arts, healing, ecology, self-expression, dress; civil, human, women's and animal rights; personal transformation and a surge of interest in things spiritual.

But I am jumping the gun. There we sat, Bob and I, that autumn evening, deploring the fact that no-one had provided us all with a simple handbook or list of ground rules for living on Earth in the hectic twentieth century. The least a soldier expects from his superiors, I observed, is training, equipment and ammunition, orders and some idea, however sketchy, of the battle ahead. So why wasn't every human being, confronted with the obstacle race called life on Earth, issued with an instruction book containing, among other things, the answers to such fundamental questions as:

'Where have I come from?'
'Why am I here?'
'What is the purpose of human existence?'
'Are unseen intelligences working alongside the human race?'
'Is there universal law? A universal Plan?'
'Where do we go from here?'

Little did Bob and I know that, at that very moment, no more than three or four miles from where we sat, that handbook was being put together, chapter by chapter!

And yet a dozen years were to pass before I happened upon segments of it, in Watkins bookshop off the Charing Cross Road in London. Having been given a grounding in various inner and outer matters by an excellent instructor who had summoned me in 1966, and having ploughed my way through acres of spiritual literature of the 400-page, door-stopper variety, I was looking for an all-purpose, everyday, uncomplicated set of instructions anyone could use as a kind of Life Primer.

My glance fell on a number of pastel-coloured booklets by someone called 'H-A' and published by The Atlanteans. I devoured them at a single sitting, and found myself revelling in their clarity, unforced sense of truth and total lack of dogma or insistence. 'H-A', an elder of the human race who had returned to guide us, if we would listen, through this crucial planetary moment, chose as his channels a small London group led by Tony Neate and, through them, began in 1957 to present a comprehensive and encouraging picture of our place in the scheme of things and of our relationship with all other forms of life.

Deeply attracted by H-A's tone of voice, I later met the Atlanteans themselves, watched their progress from Cheltenham to a lovely estate in the Malvern Hills, and eventually asked them if I might assemble some of the H-A material into a primer or guide book for today and the coming age. Tony and his companions kindly agreed, and the present volume, which owes much to the eagle eye and keen editorial mind of Ann Neate, is the outcome.

H-A has made several prophecies which time and events have since proved right. He warned us to start treating the planet with greater respect — years before the ecology movement sprang up. He was deploring male chauvinism long before the subject surfaced in our consciousness and in the media. For myself, one of H-A's most memorable remarks was his prediction in 1967 that "the time is fast coming when Merlin will awake, and the secret of wielding the sword Excalibur will once again be revealed".

Some seven years later, at the midsummer solstice, my group and I visited Park Wood at Butleigh, exact centre of the Glastonbury Zodiac where, legend has it, Merlin was last seen during his incarnation as mentor to King Arthur. In a quiet, sunlit glade in the heart of the wood, I heard Merlin's voice:

"Do not seek Excalibur on the physical plane, my son. The places where we worked still carry our vibrations, but over the centuries the true power has been stored and guarded on the higher planes. Only when groups such as yours are tuned to the highest pitch will you be able to unlock some of the power that is still available — for correct use."

Ever since, Merlin has been a source of continual encouragement, inspiration and great good humour. I find that he and H-A have much in common, and are the ultimate proof — if proof were needed — that some very distinguished helpers are rallying round us as we approach the Millennium.

If I were asked to recommend one book which will give young people — no, people everywhere of every age and circumstance — a basic understanding of our inner and outer lives, I would unhesitatingly recommend *The Guide Book*. We all need the strength, companionship and wisdom of an elder brother from time to time, and H-A is the perfect embodiment — if that is the right word! — of such a being.

Michael Dean

"How much simpler life would be if we all arrived here wearing a small book of instructions round our neck — which we could consult whenever a problem or challenge crops up. . ."
Robert Donaldson

OUR GUIDE

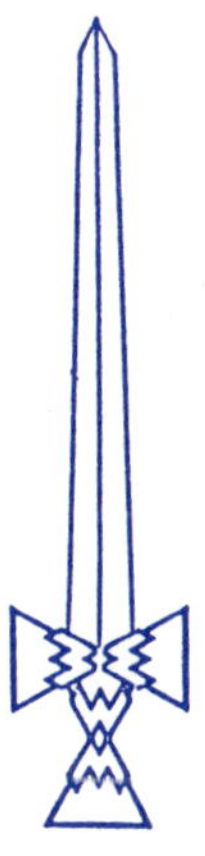

". . . a very tall presence with a tremendous sense of calm and justice all around him. Above all it was the aura and the light he emanated that I was aware of; a feeling of immense energy and power and light, yet a *complete* humility . . ."

Tony Neate's first impression of Helio-Arcanophus

1

H-A, who are you?

Accept me, my friend, for what I give out, rather than for what I might be or where I might come from. As you are well aware, an essence can only be experienced, not described. My philosophy or outlook or understanding of life is what it is. And I am what I am — no more and no less.

Just as you are kind enough to act as a channel or receiver for me, relaying my thoughts to those around you, I too act as an instrument or focus: the information and ideas I bring through to you are from many levels; that some of them can hardly be clothed in words is a limitation I hope you will accept gracefully.

If I attempted to give you any specific word-picture of my plane of existence, it would cloud or colour your conception of that plane: you would either be disappointed, or overawed.

It will always be wondered who or what I am and ever have been.

Everyone enjoys a mystery!

2

To use the modern idiom, H-A, may we ask you where you're coming from?

From a universe that contains your own and yet is part of it. And my reason for coming is to remind you of certain things you have momentarily forgotten or lost sight of — things you will need to bear in mind if you are to steer spaceship Earth through the crucial years ahead.

"What things?" you ask.

The Law, for one. Not law as you know it, but the cosmic variety.

Cosmic law holds the Universe in a state of balance and is responsible for the perpetual motion of all evolution. There are several universal laws which can be translated into terms acceptable to the human mind. Some of them are obvious, such as the law of gravity and those laws of physics which govern the relative speed and density of atoms. But there are other laws manifesting on all levels from pure thought downwards, and a failure to co-operate with them is the cause of many of the problems facing you today, both in your relationships with each other and with the Universe around you.

The forms of life you encounter on Earth are by no means the only forms of sentient and intelligent life: besides the human, there are countless variations throughout the Universe obeying the laws of adaptation to prevailing conditions — just as your own forebears adapted their bodies to the rapidly changing face of the planet during the early stages of their development. Nor does this principle apply only to physical evolution: intelligences existing on other levels — from the pure thought state downwards — also obey similar patterns.

Each species keeps to its own form of evolution, yet is a complement to the whole. Most of these are beyond the scope of your imagination, but they all stem from that ultimate Thought which generated the Universes and are bound by the directional impulses of cosmic law. Any motion against these impulses can only result in disharmony and dis-ease, both for the transgressor and for those he encounters on his backward slide.

The forward directional impulses of universal law are harmonious: they are the generators of the Love principle. This Love, or harmony, is the key to everything, for with it comes advancement and freedom from pain. Evolutionary progress through Love broadens the understanding, gives birth to wisdom and completes the perfect pattern of life on all levels.

Will that do?!

"The return of the angels to human consciousness could be one of the greatest surprises of the twentieth century. . ."

H. C. Moolenburgh, MD
A Handbook of Angels

OURSELVES

3. The Human Race Today

H-A, as a visitor to our planet, if you were commissioned to make a discreet and impartial survey of our civilisation, what would you say of the human race today?

Perhaps I could summarise it in the following way:

A highly ingenious and intelligent species, artistically accomplished, scientifically and technically advanced but, on the whole, spiritually bankrupt. By worshipping intellect, the human race has lost touch with its intuition — thereby cutting itself off from its own roots and from higher sources of guidance.

Man has not yet learned the wisdom of tolerance and respect for others who differ from him and, consequently, is fragmented into mutually antagonistic races, colours, creeds, classes and cults. As if this were not enough, man's callous indifference to the delicate biosphere on which he lives, his rape of the soil, forests, rivers, seas and the very air he breathes, have brought the planet to the brink of an even greater disaster than a world war: a total ecological breakdown.

On the plus side, growing numbers of people at last seem to be waking from their long sleep and opening their eyes to the fact that Earth which sustains you all is a rich, abundant and beautiful planet deserving better treatment than she has so far received. But the eleventh hour has long since passed: this same world has been rendered highly volatile and is in danger of suffering major devastation as a result of the actions of Superpowers misusing universal energies and principles.

A last all-out effort must now be made to alert humanity to the danger it has placed itself in, and to point out to whoever will listen the incredibly simple adjustments to human thinking and behaviour which, even now, could rescue Earth and yourselves from the jaws of impending disaster. . .

4. We are all Part of One Another

'Everything about the way our society is structured tends to separate us from each other, to label and categorise and differentiate us all. How can we possibly resist this programming and begin to see ourselves as one human family?'

It *is* difficult. But the growing planetary crisis has forced you to realise that, in a very real and practical sense, the entire human race is one organism, just one component of the biosphere Earth, alongside its many other, complementary forms of life. This is a perfect example of a positive result growing out of a negative experience, if I may say so.

Let us not dwell on such questions that immediately spring to mind as, "Why does mankind always seem to prefer to do it the hard way?" and "Why create the chaos in the first place?" Let us, instead, move back to the time before you yourselves emerged on Earth.

This is a planet which, throughout its history, has had to contend with upheavals. In the distant past these were of a natural kind, but more recently they have largely been caused by man himself.

It was hoped that, when humanity brought its influence to

bear on Earth, man, with his grasp of science and technology, would be able to complement and counterbalance the elements, and so gradually restore planetary equilibrium. Unfortunately this has not happened and we need to examine the situation to see why.

One thing that would be quite evident to any friendly observer visiting Earth is that, instead of learning to coexist with Nature, you have either tried to dominate and exploit her or you have ignored her completely. You have shown little or no respect for the other forms of life around you. You are destroying the forests, creating large areas of desert where no desert existed before; polluting the air and the oceans and rivers; draining the Earth of her resources.

If your evolution is to continue on Earth, then you urgently need to establish a rapport with the other forms of experience that are serving you so uncomplainingly. It is high time you took a long, hard look at yourselves — not as an isolated species but to see how you fit in with the terrestrial economy as a whole.

When Earth was first formed it began to experience, and part of that experience was the growing relationship between the many forms of rock, mineral and plant life and the beings of a spirit and elemental nature which assembled to guide and complement the physical nature of the planet. The aeons for which Earth has existed might seem very long to you, but when one is removed from physical life and able to put time and space into their true perspective, one realises that the Earth has been around for a comparatively short time. During that time its nature has changed, it has matured and undergone various forms of experience, just as you do.

A planetary or solar system has much in common with the structure of an atom. By far the largest component of an atom is what you would call space. Earth, then, in its relationship to the Sun, is like an electron revolving around a proton; and, in turn, the Solar System is related similarly to the galaxy. All these physical bodies and systems influence each other as they are interdependent.

What man is only just beginning to grasp is an acceptance of himself as an integral part of the whole; not just a casual appreciation, but a deep awareness on all levels, intellectual, emotional and physical, that his ideas and actions should be guided by the needs of the whole. As recent danger signals have revealed, you are each a part of the living planet and in desecrating it you are endangering yourselves.

And now, at the very moment that you are having to face all the problems you have yourselves created, the experience and evolution of the planet itself is also reaching a climax. Just as the growth of a human being is based broadly on seven-year cycles, that of the Earth occurs in approximately two-thousand-year periods, and the transition from one cycle to the next provides great opportunities for the quickening of experience and a step forward in evolution. Earth is about to come under a different form of influence: it will experience an intensified pattern of behaviour, a higher rate of spiritual metabolism.

These transitional periods are occasions when the forces of Light endeavour to present to the planet as a whole the opportunity to restore balance, the balance it is capable of achieving at such a moment of self-realisation. The only valuable experience is self-realised and, indeed, the whole process of evolution is one of self-realisation — whether it be that of the human race or of the planet itself and its many life forms, both physical and subtle.

In view of this process of unfoldment you can see that there can be no complete understanding at any one moment, only a partial understanding of the whole. In other words, you can only be what you are, no more and no less, at any one moment. This applies not only to yourselves but to any form of existence you care to consider. There is nothing negative or wrong with this state of incompletion; it is a very natural state to be in as you are continually experiencing and learning in a Universe which is infinite. You will go on for ever and ever since life is eternal.

Have you ever wondered what that means?

It is the process of eternally growing, of evolving on and on.

The one constant in this Universe is the cosmic energy of which you are a part. You are on the brink of understanding something of the nature of this energy; you do not really understand it yet, but you are beginning to acknowledge its existence. It is an energy found on every level and, as you evolve, so your keynote or vibration changes. It never stays the same. You are never the same. Every being sees from its own individual vantage point. There is nothing wrong in not seeing the whole, or even that part of it as perceived by the next person to you; the mistake you so often make is thinking that your own view is the only true one.

The negative influence that is intruding on this planet, and has been for some thousands of years, creates an atmosphere of fear and uncertainty and this is the breeding ground of greed, jealousy, aggression and the lust for power. After all, what is lust for power but the declaration of man's own feelings of inadequacy?

The key to world peace lies not in having one universal religion, it is in coming to terms with yourselves, in having the humility to accept your own incompleteness. Now that aviation and telecommunications have shrunk the world, so to speak, and put everyone in touch with everyone else, you have a priceless opportunity to realise that, despite differences of language, colour, customs and beliefs, the problems and challenges facing you all are virtually identical.

Countries are not made up of presidents, kings, prime ministers, political parties and religions — they are made of people. In some countries those people might be oppressed, yet even this is a karmic outcome of what has happened in the past.

At a personal level, you have begun to realise that good health is not related to isolated functions and dysfunctions, but to the whole person. But consider this: the way you treat everyone and everything around you reflects your true self. This is the key to good health, for health reflects your whole being.

When each and every one of you has found self-acceptance, you will begin to accept others.

Only then will you and the world be at peace.

5. Karma

Does the law of Karma operate throughout the Universe?

Certainly. Cause and effect operate throughout Creation. That is to say, every action creates a reaction. Every thought, too. ''As a man sows, so shall he reap,'' is one of the ways this law has been expressed. In other words, everything you have done and thought in the past is affecting you now, and what you are doing and thinking now is shaping your future.

Once free from the body, a spirit looks back over its record to date and, as a result, determines the sort of Earth life it next wishes to undergo. If a wise choice is made, that next life will complement all its previous lives and experiences.

No two spirits have ever trodden an identical path; each chooses its own individual way. This free choice is made by a spirit outside the body, before incarnation, because once you have been reborn as a person here on Earth, you are subject to prevailing laws, environment, national and world conditions and the many other factors that impose restrictions on the full expression of free will. This is the challenge you take on when you incarnate — to express yourself within the confines of physical life.

Do also bear in mind that not only individuals but families, groups, sects, nations and the human race as a whole are creating fresh karma, good and bad, as every minute goes by. So if the burden seems at times almost too great to bear, remember that you might be paying off not only some of your own past transgressions, but those of your previous family, group, sect or nation. And on the other hand, if you are one of those 'lucky' people who seem to be able to do no wrong, or who are always in the right place at the right time, you are probably reaping the benefit of past good deeds. From this, you will come to the conclusion that there really is no such thing as luck, but only hidden design!

It might surprise you to know that a spirit could complete its entire evolution in one lifetime, although this would be very exceptional: it usually does so during several lives — tens, hundreds or even thousands. Some spirits incarnate many times, and others very few. There is no such thing as a fixed number of incarnations, as it is up to the individual concerned.

You might meet — indeed, you might even be — a person who has returned to settle a karmic debt incurred by wrongdoing in a previous life. Such a debt can be worked off in one crucial moment, or in the first five years of life, or it may take a lifetime or even more — in which case you will have to return to 'balance the books' in yet another Earth life.

Be very careful, whatever the provocation, not to bear grudges or to harbour thoughts of revenge, for such emotional attachments will slow *you* down. Many people invoke the biblical quotation, ''An eye for an eye, a tooth for a tooth'', to justify their thirst for vengeance. This is a most unfortunate misreading of those words, which in fact mean, "By karmic law, life itself will repay every man, down to the last iota, for what he does". Whatever else you do, do not appoint yourself as judge or administrator of karmic justice. If someone wrongs you, forgive him, knowing that in due course he must reap his own reward. All thoughts of resentment, ill-will, contempt and hatred tie you to the very person or persons for whom you feel such antipathy, and eventually these karmic ties will have to be untied — by you yourself.

Remember, you chose your physical body before you entered this life. Having been born, you are still free to choose the fine details of your experience, to make the best or worst of your life, to fulfil it or to let it drift aimlessly — or even to embark on a career of cruelty, selfishness and destruction.

And you are making that choice every day.

Remember also, Fate is *not* some blind, capricious, illogical force that goes around impulsively bestowing its favours and punishments at random. Fate is the outcome of personal, family, group, national and racial events.

You are at liberty, during your present life, to modify, soften and shape the future; to mould your destiny, in fact.

6. The First Seven Years of Childhood

We usually think of conception, birth and early childhood in purely physical terms. Would you give us an insight into these processes from your own point of view?

Gladly. As I have said, throughout the ages you have tended to place the ultimate responsibility for your destiny either on a god of some kind or on an even more capricious and unreliable entity called Fate. Whereas, as you know, the law of Karma places the responsibility fairly and squarely on your *own* shoulders.

Another law operating throughout the Universe guarantees each of you the free will to evolve in the manner and at the speed you choose. The evidence to support this statement is all around you — man can and does do what he wishes. He can explore, create or destroy. He can vegetate, drift with the current, sidetrack or backtrack. I ask you to bear this firmly in mind, because in this fundamental principle lies the very essence of what I have to say; indeed, my entire outlook on life as it is unfolding here on Earth and elsewhere is built around this law of *self*-determination.

We live in an expanding Universe, one in which the Creator or First Cause is continuously giving out fresh thought or energy or spirit. (How inadequate are words to describe this mighty enterprise!) That thought goes out and experiences by virtue of its own free will, and yet it is part of the Creator itself; so in effect, God is perpetually experiencing through subtle planes and dimensions, physical galaxies, suns, planets, Nature, man, particles, atoms — throughout all Creation. When each spirit completes its cycle of growth and evolution and returns to that from which it emerged, it takes its own wisdom and experience with it. Thus the Godhead itself is forever evolving in its own infinite wisdom.

And now to specifics:

Let us say that a spirit decides to reincarnate on Earth. It chooses a body that offers it the circumstances it requires to complement the experiences it has already had. The spirit enters that body *at the moment of conception*. On this point I must be adamant, because there can be no physical life whatsoever without spirit. As soon as the human seed has germinated there is spirit, make no mistake about it.

While the baby is growing in its mother's womb, the foetus and the spirit within it assume equal importance, and are directly affected by the mother's health and way of life. Which brings us to the grim fact that every day most of you are inhaling harmful gases and chemicals from vehicles and factories, and eating still more chemicals and preservatives in your food. Indeed, the human body today is being subjected to abuses for which it was not designed. This concerns me deeply, because the effects of this abuse are not necessarily felt in a single generation.

The human body can only adapt or mutate slowly, so the various poisons that you are now inflicting on your bodies are creating major problems for the future. Such unnatural conditions will inevitably take effect sooner or later. Even six months prior to the conception of a child, both the mother and the father should pay special attention to their diet and all excesses should be avoided, so serious is the responsibility. They should eat sensibly and live sensibly, especially during the period of incubation — a time when the incarnating spirit inside the mother is struggling to come to terms with its small and comparatively helpless body and will be grateful for whatever mental, emotional and spiritual nourishment its mother and, indirectly, its father can provide.

When the baby is born, it begins to express itself physically. During these early days it is still aware, at the back of its mind, of what happened before; not in the sense that it can recall specific episodes or events and convey them to you, although this has been known to happen, but in the sense that the essence of what it experienced in past lives is still with it.

During the child's first two years, its parents help it to become aware of its physical senses — to feel, to taste, to smell, to see and to hear. These means of impression and expression which the adult takes for granted are new experiences to that child. Faces, colours, shapes, sounds, smells and tones of voice are already making their mark, helping to determine the kind of person the child will eventually become.

As the child learns to speak and to communicate, it lives and delights in 'a world of its own'. It sees and experiences subtle planes of existence — the spirits of the Nature kingdoms, for example — which adults have long since put aside as 'imagination'. It loves to explore a world it can create for itself, to enjoy adventures and fantasies that need have no outer reality. What *is* reality? Is it what the spirit within you senses? Whatever resonates through every fibre of your being? Or is it everyday life?

To you, an adult, reality is the chair you sit in, the floor you stand on, the meals you eat, the bills you pay. But before you came into your physical body, what was reality then? It was your thoughts and emotions and memories and all that you had experienced previously. It was colour, light, sound, the ability to look at a situation and without analysing or computing it, to know it, to *be* it. To be where your mind takes you, with no space or time to slow the process. *This* is the reality the child brings with it. So during these early years, I urge you not to stifle this wonderful openness, this crucial phase when your child is using senses that are as natural and intrinsic to its spirit as the physical senses are to its body.

As it enters the second phase of these first seven years, at the age of three or four, the child needs contact with other children. This is a time when relationships beyond the immediate family circle should be encouraged, in order to increase its experience of the world outside that protective circle. It is also a time when the child's intelligence and imagination should be developed. But I do not recommend anyone to cram a child's mind intellectually, because the growing process should be gradual and balanced with every other activity. Grow a flower in a hothouse and overfeed it with fertiliser and you might get an extra-large flower, but it will probably have a weak stem and, if so, will soon wither.

And so it is with a human being. A child should be allowed to grow slowly and surely so that it has a strong stem, a firm foundation on which to build its life. Then it will unfold gradually, and when, like a flower, it comes to bloom, it will be sturdy and well-balanced yet have a sensitivity and harmony with everything around it.

Needless to say, these first seven years of life are of the utmost importance. The emotional link between parents and child at this time is crucial, as parents are in almost every instance the only certainty the child can cling to; the only source of food, love, protection; the only means of survival.

And what of discipline?

A hotly debated subject that has always bred extremes of opinion.

Shall we approach it from a broad perspective? Which, as I am sure you have already noted, I sometimes prefer to do!

The Universe, as your astronomers and other scientists will confirm, is an orderly Universe: you can see it from the natural laws operating everywhere around you, without which nothing would hold together but would fly apart into random currents of energy. In such a Universe you have to play the game, you have to observe the ground rules. Jump off a roof, and you fall. Put a finger in the fire, and it burns. Stay out in the snow and ice, and you freeze.

You also need to develop some corresponding order or discipline within yourself — otherwise you will find yourself struggling against the natural flow of things, unable to follow your own directional impulse that will help your spirit find its true expression. If a child is not given some sort of solid framework in which to live, it will in all probability go haywire

— because it has no yardstick, no guidelines, no foundation on which to stand. It might even lose the impetus and direction of its life, and so waste an entire incarnation.

And when, in turn, this young person grows up and has children of its own, the process continues, culminating in a society with little sense of direction, deteriorating standards, with no beliefs, no sense of purpose and no confidence in its own future.

If this rather grim scenario seems to describe what is already happening here, now, on Earth — then you will know just how crucial each and every parent/child relationship is to the stability of your entire civilisation.

I hasten to add, however, that discipline should never be forced on a child by intolerance or impatience. Nor should you ever punish a child or resent it for intruding on your time and space — because *you* summoned it into time and space in the first place!

No-one, of course, child or parent, is perfect; the mother and father who never raised hand or voice to their child has never lived. But as a child grows it *needs* those guidelines, because not until it reaches maturity can the spirit 'come in close' and establish a sound relationship with the physical body — and so influence it more directly, according to its own level of wisdom.

It is for this reason, rather than for any other, that you should give your children a fundamental sense of what is right and what is wrong. You might argue that standards change, that attitudes towards morality are continually evolving. True. But there are certain principles, unwritten rules, which have always worked and always will, for the benefit and protection of all. These are constants, and I think anyone who is honest with himself will admit that, without them, human society would collapse into anarchy and chaos.

To those of you who still insist that from the earliest age a child should be allowed to do or say anything it chooses, at any time, I shall reply, "That way lies total freedom, yes. But, human nature being what it is, that expression can range from the most inspired and creative to the most selfish and destructive and, ultimately, self-destructive." And so I submit that the interests of everyone will be served if:

> you give your infant love and care,
> you encourage it to develop its imagination and sensitivity,
> you gently teach it self-discipline and the boundaries of behaviour,
> you give it a grounding in self-respect, relationships with and responsibility towards others,
> and, finally you encourage it to develop and express the talents and aptitudes it undoubtedly possesses.

7. The Second Seven Years: 8 to 14

Planet Earth is a university spiralling through an ocean of mind. You come aboard so that you can experience some of the rewards and limitations of life on the physical plane. You spend much of your first seven years on board trying to get used to the rather cumbersome space-suit provided — your physical body. Such is the Earth's atmosphere that this space-suit, with its various functions and attachments, including an automatic respiratory system, has to be worn at all times of the day. (At night, you are allowed to leave the campus, but that is a subject we shall look at later.)

Some colleges in this university are run on strict, repressive lines, but in most of them, fortunately, the syllabus is very flexible and you can take virtually any subject you choose; you can study hard or free-wheel and take your leisure. Only when you finally leave the university do you have to take an examination. But here is some extraordinary news: *you mark your own papers* — no-one else does! And you decide when and if you will go back for another course, and what subjects you will take when you do.

This is why you have to face up to all the problems and challenges that life on Earth offers you, for when you finally arrive at your disembarkation point, you take with you all you have learned, and a mental list of all the tests you failed or avoided.

For the first seven years, as I have said, you are finding your feet in your new surroundings — with the help, one hopes, of a loving family and friends. You are developing your imagination, beginning to explore a new and unfamiliar world.

In my opinion, it is not until the child reaches the age of seven that you should start its formal education, because before that time you will be denying the spirit of the child the opportunity to learn from its imagination.

The next seven years are equally important, but for a different reason. This is the time when the spirit and the physical body are carried forward into puberty, and a child becomes increasingly aware of its relationship to other children and to adults. It begins to emerge from that private world where its thoughts and ideas were more important and more real to it than the 'real' world outside; now its inner adventures become less real than its outer life.

This can be a difficult time for the child, as it realises it has to begin to cope with physical and material problems — and that no-one else can see into or understand the private world it is gradually leaving.

During the period from eight to fourteen, the child begins to analyse not only itself but those around it; its critical faculties start to develop and it no longer believes everything it is told. Parents and teachers should be very patient, and careful not to fob the child off with silly answers to direct questions, because the child will quickly see through evasive or embarrassed answers. It will begin to lose confidence in those it trusts and depends on and, if that happens, insecurity can develop and psychological problems take root.

During this period too, parents are faced with the difficult problem of teaching their child self-discipline. Difficult, yes, but ultimately rewarding, because if you *can* teach your child self-discipline, it will almost invariably develop self-respect, then respect for others. And the best way to teach anyone is by example: the process must start with the parents themselves.

Of course, a child will be influenced by other children and fashion and pressure from the media, so there will be times when it will rebel against you, against its school, against all sorts of things; but all these rebellions are only symptoms of a spirit trying to find self-expression through the physical body. It is a period of intense frustration because the body is still growing and is unable to respond fully to the impulses of the spirit — with results that every parent knows. If the spirit is strong, the frustration will be all the more.

I urge all parents to *accept* this phase of rebellion that allows the intense child to emerge from the cocoon and establish its own identity. This restless energy is sometimes interpreted as lack of discipline, lack of respect, or the parents' inability to cope with the child. Often it is none of these things, but simply the turbulence of a spirit, either unable to find self-expression in barren or restrictive surroundings, or simply kicking against authority in order to find its individuality.

If parents were to spend a few minutes each night thinking — not worrying — about their children, it would pay handsome dividends. A child could be likened to a highly complex piece of machinery controlled by a computer so subtle and so sensitive that the slightest shock can send it off-balance. So, every night, why not say to yourself, ''This is my child; it has chosen me to be its parent, to care for it. I am going to work hard to help its spirit and physical body to achieve a harmony.'' Send your child a positive thought of love, see the thought envelop it, and this too will help the balancing and aligning process. I am confident that if you do this every night, and whenever you feel conflict going on within your child, your unseen labours will be rewarded.

This is a time in your child's life when it is really seeking. Give it as varied a life-diet as possible, because during this period the seeds are being sown for its activities and interests later. From the age of fourteen onwards it will begin to build on the experiences it has undergone during the previous seven years, so try to give your child as much encouragement as possible. It might not always respond to the various options you offer it, but remember that it is still exploring and uncertain, and is likely to regard complying with *your* suggestions as a surrender of its own individuality.

Don't despair, just see that your child's creative imagination is stimulated and that the experience you offer it is as wide and deep as you can possibly make it. For this reason — and also because most children during this period tend to want to live beyond their capacities — please make sure your child gets plenty of sleep. Experience will soon tell you how much is needed. See that the child has enough sleep for its particular character and physical make-up because, apart from the physical processes that are taking place, it is during sleep that the spirit leaves the body to receive tuition and experiences in other realms. These are most important if the child is to be refreshed and revitalised for the next day. There is a huge reservoir of collective human experience, folklore, tradition and knowledge available to any young person sensitive enough to tap it during sleep.

From the parents' point of view, these seven years from eight to fourteen should be the most exciting ones, for you will see greater changes then than at any other period in your child's life. You will see your child emerge from the period of almost total imagination into a phase when reality begins to intrude; you will watch it forming relationships with others, beginning to develop its ability to analyse, becoming aware of its physical body and approaching adulthood, stage by stage. There is a tremendous range of evolutionary dramas to participate in, and every child needs a lot of understanding and, above all, patience, from those who guide it.

A child is a very sensitive organism and the relationship between its spirit and body — forgive me for stressing and repeating this — is very delicately balanced. I do not recommend physical forms of punishment, or mental or emotional punishment, for wayward or disobedient children. These reprisals might succeed in getting the anger out of the adult's system but, in doing so, transfer it to the child. In my view, the adult who resorts to physical punishment or mental or emotional reprisals is admitting his own failure to come to terms with that child.

A child has nothing but love to offer — despite the fact that it can be mischievous, perverse and destructive; despite the fact that, in trying to express itself, it will often do things that seem intolerable to you. And if it does, ask yourself what could lie behind a young person's violence, anger and apparent self-destructiveness?

There is no blame, only cause.

The more love you can give a child, the more healing it will receive at every level. This is possibly the most important factor to consider, so don't be embarrassed to show your children affection, whether you are parent, teacher or friend. Girls and boys alike need warmth and love and physical contact, because all these will help their inner and outer selves to align. Often you can do more to repair a situation with that contact, with a flow of warmth and affection and understanding, than in any other way.

8. Approaching Adulthood: 15 to 21

And the next seven years?

Let me first summarise what we have just discussed:

When a spirit enters its chosen body at the moment of conception, it is setting out on a new adventure. It brings with it all its previous experience, assembled now in that one speck of physical life. And as that spirit enters the fertilised seed, the process of incarnation has begun. The seed develops into an embryo and gradually the spirit starts to manipulate that tiny body. For the spirit well knows that if its incarnation is to be fruitful, then it has to come to terms with this new physical body in which it has set up house.

The prenatal period, as I have said, is crucial, as it is a time of adjustment, a necessary preparation for birth. Up to that moment the tiny body has had the protection of its own aura and that of the mother who bears it. There are few more beautiful sights than that of a mother-to-be glowing with the knowledge of what she is experiencing, and instinctively aware of the responsibility of introducing another being to the planet. She is enriched, as she not only has her own spirit, but another blending with her own — one that is just starting out on the adventure of life.

It is because of the sympathy between these two spirits that the relationship between mother and child is quite different from that between child and father. The father has not carried the child inside him. On the other hand it may well be that he and his child have been together before and so he feels, subconsciously, a memory stirring. That can work two ways, of course: sometimes it is a memory of harmony and love, while in other instances, it may be a sense of disharmony and even enmity — in which case the child might be returning to attempt to resolve the problem. All too often, unaware of the hostility or incompatibility that developed between them in a previous life, two people will continue to clash in the present life, so the problem intensifies rather than diminishes. And *all* discord, whether it is between individuals, families, groups, sects and nations, has to be resolved in due course.

The spirit within you in infancy is strong because it has to initiate, to break through and supervise the productive mechanisms of the physical body. It has to make you function. So you will appreciate how much more there is to the growth of a child than mere chemical and physical processes.

For the first seven years a child is becoming aware; it is gathering new experiences, thoughts, tastes. Then in the next period it begins to ask why, to rationalise. No longer can it accept everything the parents have to say and offer. It begins to think beyond them.

These seven-year periods are, of course, only approximate: young people vary enormously, some developing with astonishing speed, others maturing more slowly.

We are now approaching one of the most difficult phases in the life of a growing human being. Why? Because this is the time when brain and body assume a dominance over the spirit; a time of inner conflict when parents' guidance should be very sensitive and sympathetic. The young person's physical brain has reached a certain stage of maturity; it has acquired a vocabulary and has already started to reason and question more deeply; the body's reproductive system has begun to function. The young person has to come to terms with all these developments. Many also find that on certain subjects they can think rings round their parents, which can add to the confusion.

How can a child best be helped during this difficult phase? You can be sure that there will be times when the balance between the various processes goes haywire — when the body develops in one direction, the emotions in another, the mind in a third and the spirit . . . well, that might be around somewhere, trying hard to keep the peace! And not only the child's own spirit but others that are trying to help it during this crisis period are having a very difficult time indeed.

During adolescence you must bear in mind that your child is beginning to break away from your aura completely. Until now, the connecting link between you has gradually been dissolving. At the age of fourteen that link is severed and the child suddenly has a feeling of being on its own. This applies even in the closest and happiest of families.

At first this is a marvellous thing because the young person can see, enjoy and do many of the things that adults do. And then it becomes aware of being alone. Sometimes this sense of isolation can manifest as fear or introversion; at others, it can express itself as a kicking out and rebelling against society.

All you can do at such a time is to offer, without strings or other attachments and conditions, endless patience, love and — if it can be accepted — guidance; and to recognise that your son or daughter is now a person in his or her own right.

You cannot expect your child to grow up in the way *you* want it to, because that child needs to unfold in its own individual way. No-one in a physical body can wholly understand another's karma: you can only see from your own particular viewpoint and the most frequent mistake of parents is to expect and even insist on certain things of their child, instead of being grateful for what the child truly is.

Each child born into this world has a unique spirit and appearance and character; it is going to think and react differently from everyone else. At this time, all over the world, many highly evolved spirits are coming into physical bodies, which means that they are having a more difficult time than others coming to terms with the physical shell.

I believe that this is not only a period of great potential enlightment and therefore a challenge for parents, teachers and leaders alike, but also a most significant time in the history of the planet and the human race, and that we must do everything in our power to rise to the occasion.

9. Parents and Children

I have tried hard to understand my children, but whatever I say or suggest they seem to reject — simply because I am their parent. Can you help me to understand and accept this?

You have my every sympathy. So often, because the young as a whole feel betrayed by their elders, individual parents, though loving and caring, are finding themselves dismissed and rejected by children who would, if only they stopped to reflect for a moment, do quite the opposite. This is a classic case of throwing the parent out with the bath-water!

Maybe it will lessen your dismay a little if we detach ourselves for a moment from your own experience and look at things from the perspective of recent history:

After the last World War, with all its attendant horrors and sacrifices, most thinking people determined to replace the destructive policies and attitudes that had made the war possible, so that coming generations would have a better chance of security and peace. And now, some forty years later, we are in a position to look back and ask ourselves if those good intentions have borne fruit.

But what do we see? Around us we see a new generation which feels utterly alien from its elders, and is consequently intolerant and impatient with them.

"Is *this* the world you have been trying so hard to create?" the young are exclaiming. "If so, we want no part of it."

And, in many respects, who can blame them? Today's parents cannot be blamed either — for they too were children not so long ago, and are the product of their own parents in turn. Yet the fact remains that, if a child is to be able to express himself and begin to develop a positive, outgoing nature, he must have a background of some stability, emotionally and otherwise. He must be able to respect his parents, and they him. He must have some form of spiritual heritage, one which can prepare him to cope with the hazards and challenges of modern life.

The young must be encouraged to see that their inner and outer lives are one; that these are not split into two unrelated compartments — one a mythical ideal confined to Sundays and the other a harsh, workaday reality. *This* is the attitude, the dangerous delusion of separation, that has to be broken down.

If we are to help young people to express themselves — and to prepare for adulthood and parenthood — we must pass on to them a basis of self-discipline and self-respect, because these and these alone will create the foundation or framework of their lives, and lead automatically to such other essentials as respect for others and for the planet which supplies their every need.

As the age of secrecy, intrigue and oppression dies away — and you can feel it disintegrating as mankind's hunger for the truth grows — you must nourish the young with the basic universal truths, but not necessarily one set of beliefs to the exclusion of all others, for that way lies the fanaticism and dogma which have stained human history for so long.

You must also be prepared to let your children enlighten you: many youngsters of today are bringing with them skills and insights that make their parents seem positively slow by comparison.

Any intelligent child, unforced and unconditioned, will recognise the designing Intelligence behind all life, and this realisation alone will lead to all the doors an enquiring young mind could wish to open.

It is a privilege for parents to have children. Morally the child owes you nothing and, despite the admitted sacrifices and self-denial that parenthood entails — and these are themselves initiations you will one day be glad to have undergone — you have no right to pressure your children, to demand affection from them, to tie them to you or to expect them to model their lives or occupations or careers on your own.

Whatever love, respect or loyalty you receive from your children will be earned: it can never be insisted upon or forced. Force will only result in fear and loathing. Smother, repress or torture your child, and in the fullness of time you will reap what you have sown, for such is the law of inevitable consequence, the Law of Karma. Love and cherish and protect your child, and you too will enjoy similar blessings in days to come. This again is the great Law in action.

Forgive me for having dwelt so long on various negative aspects of this engrossing subject, but I think you will agree that they must be faced if we are to turn the situation round. That having been said, I would like to suggest that, despite the present alienation being felt by both the young and their parents alike, parenthood is possibly the most important, skilled and potentially rewarding occupation in all human life.

How very strange, then, that this vital subject seems to be ignored by your schools, colleges and universities. . .

10. Man, Woman and the Law of Polarity

Although we are physically either female or male, our spirits are presumably neither — or both?

The spirit inhabiting your body is sexless in your understanding of the word. In fact it is androgynous. In one incarnation a spirit may choose to experience through a male body, and in the next a female. Nevertheless, that spirit is itself a duality, positive/negative, and *only one* of these two aspects animates each human being: the other remains in higher worlds.

If a spirit goes seriously off balance, one of two fundamental things can happen — it can either overemphasise its ego and see itself as a master in its own eyes, or it can become apathetic and lose its desire to evolve. An overemphasised ego can therefore be taken as a spiritual danger signal, as can an introverted rejection of life's flow. You will see from this how vital it is to maintain a balance between your spirit and your physical body — and for your spirit to endeavour to reconcile the two facets of itself.

Let us now relate this question of polarity to men and women. You may well ask what happens when a man and woman marry. Should marriage be necessary, apart from the purpose of procreation? First let us take a spirit that enters a male body. The male body tends to encourage spiritual apathy, partly as a result of a preoccupation with material matters. This is why, from an evolutionary point of view, a male incarnation can hold the spirit back unless it is strong enough to resist this tendency. Conversely, in most women the spirit is accentuated and this fosters a more compassionate nature — and, of course, the maternal instinct.

This phenomenon has been neatly expressed in the saying: "Men *do*, women *are*."

What of a good marriage, a good union between two people? I use the word 'union' because a marriage by civil or even religious rites is not necessarily a spiritual marriage in the eyes of God. The Divine sanction can only fall on a union in which there is a true affinity on all levels. If two people are joined together and they love and understand each other spiritually, mentally and physically, thereby finding contentment, relaxation, friendship and unselfishness on all these levels, they are in fact aiding the evolutionary balance of their own spirits. When two people enjoy such a union, the predominance of the various facets in both sexes are balanced out. You will probably find that they both have a broad outlook on life and an understanding and tolerance, not only of themselves but of the world around them.

For those who do not find a life partner, it can be a little more difficult to achieve this balance between the two facets of the spirit. But remaining single is infinitely preferable to being enmeshed in an unsuccessful marriage, and many single people find a counterbalance to their personality and spirit in a close friend or relative.

All men and women have both masculine (outgoing, rational) and feminine (receptive, intuitive) sides to their nature to a greater or lesser degree and the ideal is to keep a reasonable balance and not allow one side of your character to become overexaggerated. Know yourself for what you are, recognise your virtues and your limitations and you will be making all the progress you or anyone else could wish for during this particular lifetime.

The most serious, indeed dangerous, flaws in a male-dominated society are not only that men are reluctant to consult women and to benefit from the wisdom and experience and instinct of women, but also that men themselves suppress the gentler, feminine aspects of their *own* nature.

On the other hand, women need to watch that they don't over-react and allow the outgoing, masculine side of their nature to swing the balance to the other extreme, for in so doing they are in danger of losing their essential femininity.

On all levels of your being you have the challenge of maintaining balance, for it is the extremes that will topple you. Don't *push* yourself on any level. Don't try to be *perfect* — you wouldn't be here if you were! Acknowledge your strengths and weaknesses, and try to walk the midway path of poise and equilibrium.

11. Sleep

Sleep is largely uncharted territory. Could you throw a little light on it for us?

You know why sleep is necessary for the physical body. But what of the spirit? Rest is as essential to the spirit as to the body and, while the body sleeps, the spirit leaves it and enters the inner planes where it is recharged with cosmic energy. If your sleep is disturbed, your spirit body does not get the proper chance to recharge and, consequently, the next day you are not only tired physically but also rather far away and out of focus.

The spirit is connected etherically to the body in two places: at the head and the solar plexus. A clairvoyant who is able to see the spirit projected away from the body will notice the silver cord connecting them.

During sleep your spirit will do one of three things — it will either stay with your body, hover near it, or travel away to other places and dimensions. It may journey to foreign countries or even to other planets to gain knowledge that will supplement the experience it is gaining on the Earth plane. If a group of spirits are trying to achieve a particular task in the world, they sometimes meet on the inner planes to generate a greater thought force or spiritual momentum for their work. There are many kinds of work and experience available to the spirit while the body is asleep, and each spirit will undertake whatever is in keeping with its own development. For instance, after recharging itself on the inner planes, a spirit might do healing or rescue work, attend a place of learning, visit loved ones, seek advice from guides and instructors, or even take part in a particular project or mission.

But for all this wealth of activity, there are certain things that can only be experienced in the physical body, and this is why you incarnate in the first place. Ideally, a balance should be struck between your daily adventures on Earth and those undergone on the inner planes during your sleep.

From all this you will appreciate why you sometimes feel momentarily stunned if you have been woken suddenly out of a deep sleep: your spirit has been too abruptly recalled from its inner work and activity.

12. Dreams and Astral Travel

How do we know whether we have had a dream or an astral experience?

Before answering, may I point out that although the term 'astral' is often loosely used to denote all the various inner planes it should, strictly speaking, only apply to the thought planes nearest to the physical world and *not* to the spirit realms beyond.

To begin with dreams: the subconscious mind is a vast storehouse, a highly efficient computer that records your every thought, feeling and action, whether good, bad or indifferent. When you dream, your subconscious mind brings forward a set of experiences to your conscious mind, most of which are forgotten when you wake.

Sometimes dreams are merely concerned with the surface conscience, the conscience that is influenced by social environment and pressures. Such dreams can act as a safety valve for tensions and repressions, helping to adjust a mind that has been subjected to frustration or some other form of stress. At other times, deep inner messages from your spirit can surface in dreams, using the symbolic language of imagery from the subconscious and acting as clarifying or even healing agents.

The interpretation of dreams is no easy matter. First you must distinguish between the wheat and the chaff — the significant part of the dream and the irrelevant — then interpret its symbolism or inner meaning. And, remember, you the dreamer should, as far as possible, interpret your own dreams; they can be an invaluable aid to understanding your inner problems.

Sometimes while you sleep, your spirit might try to bring something through to your conscious brain in the form of a message or warning or other communication from another plane. A psychic person will more easily be able to remember this kind of premonitory dream, as the link between spirit and conscious mind will be clearer.

Many people experience unconscious astral travel during sleep when their astral body leaves the physical and they are able to re-call the sensation of flying or visiting far-off places. As for *conscious* astral projection which some people practice, what shall I say? It can be hazardous, even dangerous, if not learned under the guidance of an experienced and responsible teacher — and even then should only be practised for selfless purposes.

Experience of other dimensions during sleep is an involuntary projection of the spirit onto the inner planes for the purpose of learning or helping in one way or another. It is involuntary in the sense that the mind does not consciously cause the projection. As the spirit is involved, the motivation originates from the inner rather than the surface conscience and will be determined by the evolutionary state of the spirit concerned. These experiences usually have a feeling of clarity and logic; but again, they may not be strictly logical by Earth standards, coming as they do from a dimension for which there are no terms of reference in Earth language.

These are the principal differences between:

a dream or subconscious release,
unconscious astral travel,
experience of the higher planes.

It is up to you to learn to distinguish between the three for yourself. The feeling you experience when your spirit returns to your body after visiting other planes is unmistakable. As an experiment, may I suggest that when you wake every day, you try to determine whether you have been dreaming, astrally travelling, or visiting the spirit worlds. With practice, you will soon recognise the differences.

You can also, before falling asleep, determine to remember your dreams when you wake. As with any other skill, the immediate results will probably be less than perfect, but persist and eventually you will be rewarded.

13. Meditation

What is the point of meditation?

In this modern world, where the advantages of periods of quietness are fast being denied you, there is a growing need for a form of meditation that is easily adaptable to the western lifestyle and which, at the same time, affords the meditator an opportunity to open the door that leads to his own inner landscape.

I have, therefore, suggested a meditation course[*] of simple mental and physical exercises designed to give a growing awareness of the mind, body and nervous system that can help every one of you in your daily life and also aid those who have a psychic aptitude to handle it constructively and responsibly.

In the West, until recently, meditation has been thought

---

[*]MEDITATION — A basic course in three parts: Devised and published by The Atlanteans, Runnings Park, Croft Bank, West Malvern, Worcestershire WR14 4BP, England. (£3.95 plus 60p p&p)

by many to be merely an abstract exercise, but in the East it represents a method of achieving awareness on many levels, a progression and extension of your entire being.

In its true sense, meditation is not the self-centred withdrawal that some would have you believe, but a real form of service and a positive contribution to your fellow men. It is up to each of you who meditates to decide how far you are able to achieve this.

The first thing to consider before embarking upon a course of meditation is whether you direct your own life. Are you your own master, the charioteer of your soul, or do you simply flow along with the crowd and let others do your thinking for you? The calm afforded by divorcing oneself from a serious problem, even if only for a few minutes, can go a long way towards solving it. The body, emotions and mind relax and allow the spirit to come closer, strengthening its link with the physical vehicle.

Meditation is also a tool to enable you to be more creative, more objective, to improve relationships, to find greater harmony with the planet and other kingdoms and to aid the expansion of consciousness so that the path of self-realisation may unfold for you. It will help you to establish your identity and release your full potential.

14. The Aura

Is it true that everyone has an aura?

Every spirit in a human body has an aura, as also does every living being. It is an etheric substance surrounding the physical shell, protecting it from the full impact of cosmic forces and shielding it from unwanted influences such as hostile thoughts and other people's negative emotion, and even from germs and viruses. If the physical body and its counterpart the etheric body had not this protective envelope, they would be open to attack from all quarters and would certainly not survive.

Your aura reflects your physical, mental, emotional and spiritual state moment by moment and can sometimes be seen by those with 'second sight'. A healthy and balanced person would have an aura that is strong and well aligned. One of the tasks of a healer is to cleanse, strengthen and adjust this subtle energy.

To take responsibility for your own aura, you must first realise that it is a thought emanation from your spirit. As such, it is easily controlled by thought — your own thought. Simply imagine yourself encased in a cocoon of light that is whole and perfect. You can think of it as an unbroken force-field circling round you, a blue or white light emanating from you, or you may sense it as a sphere or bubble that surrounds you. These are visualising aids, but the essential discipline is to keep your aura closed, especially in the head area, by the power of your own thought. Simply think it!

This simple exercise will not seal you off from harmonious energies in the cosmos but it will help you maintain an inner balance on all levels.

15. Can Anyone Heal?

Just as anyone can sing, so can anyone channel healing energy. It is a form of human expression. But as some sing better than others, so are some more suited to giving healing than others.

Basically, healing is the channelling of cosmic or divine energy to another person to enable his or her spirit to adjust its own unbalanced energy patterns. With training it is possible to tackle all kinds of dis-ease, physical, psychological and even disturbed mental states, although the latter require a much more specialised knowledge and experience.

Remember, though, that receiving benefit from healing is only one side of the picture. Your patients will need to contribute to their own recovery in a conscious way if they do not wish to fall ill again. This means paying attention to diet and nutrition, the type of food they eat, and how it is prepared and grown. It also means becoming aware of their attitude to themselves, to others and to life itself. In other words, true healing is about an holistic approach to life and health and may sometimes need to embrace both orthodox and com-plementary therapies.

So if you are learning the art of healing, you should also develop a broad approach to the whole subject and acquire some skill in listening and counselling, referring your patients to other therapists or specialists when necessary.

True healing requires dedication and humility on the part of the healer and can only take place in the patient when it is accompanied by a growth of understanding.

Healing Courses organised by the Atlanteans are held at Runnings Park, Croft Bank, West Malvern, WR14 4BP and in other parts of the United Kingdom

16. Education Today, Long Ago and Tomorrow

Our educational system is in a state of upheaval and change. What direction should education take in the future?

Everywhere around you there are young people of talent, energy, originality, even genius, whose individual growth is frustrated; and there are teachers who are equally frustrated through a lack of creativity in their work and an inability to take a personal interest in their individual pupils, for whatever reason.

Education in much of your world today has become too specialised, too factual and too segmented. It has tended to narrow, rather than widen, the perspective of its pupils and emphasise the divisions, rather than the correlations, between the various aspects of life. So that knowledge, instead of being appreciated as a whole made up of many facets, is presented as many separate and somewhat unrelated subjects.

Your youth is your future. Education, therefore, needs to

be given top priority and teaching become the distinguished career that it really should be.

Thousands of years ago in Atlantis, teachers — like priests and kings — were people who had a real vocation and whose spiritual status alone qualified them for their work. While a child was still young, its parents would take it to the temple where adepts, having read the child's aura, would decide which occupation or profession would best suit it. Those selected for teaching were then trained in the temple by men and women of great understanding, intelligence and wisdom.

The young person was taught gradually, as any form of intense cramming is undesirable. It was understood in those days that if, at a young age, the mental ability is encouraged to move forward too quickly, it can leave the development of the emotional nature behind and a brilliant, but emotionally immature, adult emerges.

The practicalities of life were taught as well as academic subjects and, instead of learning parrot fashion, the young were encouraged to think for themselves. This was considered most important for any young person training to teach others later in life.

And what of today? It is true that some schools take pride in devoting themselves to the personal development of their students, encouraging individuality and nurturing talent as it emerges; but they are few and far between. . . I would like to suggest some changes of emphasis that would greatly benefit the youth of today and, of course eventually, mankind of tomorrow.

First, your educational system needs to cater for physical,

mental, emotional *and* spiritual needs. It is these last two areas, especially, that need a more enlightened attitude.

Secondly, a child should be allowed to discover its own natural level in relation to others, without the pressure of forced competition as a spur to efforts. So often this achieves either an inflated ego or a damaging lack of confidence and self-worth.

Thirdly, during the formative years at school, a child's creative imagination needs to be stimulated to help it to unfold naturally from within, like a plant; so that later in life it can work cooperatively with others and contribute its own creative input.

These are a few guidelines. Yet, the responsibility of a balanced educational system must also rest on the shoulders of parents and on those responsible for the economic system.

For instance, it is important for a parent not to live out his or her ambition through the child, but to allow it to develop at its own pace and in its own way. Equally, there is a need for those in government to rise above the concept of creating 'cannon fodder' for a particular segment of industry at the expense of the broader aspects of a holistic education. Over-specialisation is not successful and the cramping of a young person's outlook is a fatal trap. We need a world that has time for other people's points of view and beliefs. Thus freedom of thought and open-mindedness has to start at the beginning — with the educational system.

When the present methods of education give way to a more compassionate and far-sighted system, then education will be seen for what it really should be: a magical mystery tour in which the various wonders of life and the planet on which you live are revealed; in which spiritual understanding and values are encouraged, not sneered at, and pupils are appreciated as individuals growing in awareness, as thoughts of God.

And when that happens, as it surely will in the not-too-distant future, life will no longer be an obstacle race you have to run while wearing a blindfold — but an exhilarating adventure that has no end and no limitations.

17. Money, Money, Money

Money has become one of our major preoccupations: most people seem to be pursuing not wisdom or achievement or even fulfilment, but money. It has even become abstract, illusory — paper chasing paper, promises, collateral, spirals of make-believe. Mind games, power games . . .

Yes, but this is hardly surprising, is it? A race of people cut off from its own roots and origins, believing in nothing it cannot see and touch and weigh, requires status symbols to measure its achievements. And so money has outgrown its original purpose.

Since earliest times you have used various forms of metal as a means of exchange, as there is something about metallic elements that exerts a strange fascination. Precious stones too, their value being determined by their rarity, colour, cut and brilliance. When you hold a diamond in your hand, you become aware of something rather special about the stone, because the element within it gives off a type of power or vibration which affects you, however subtly. Some dealers can tell a diamond purely by its feel, by holding it to their skin. What they may not realise is that they are picking up the vibration of that stone and of the life-force or intelligence within it. If it were made of glass or paste it would not have the same feel, the same vibration.

Centuries ago people who were interested in the mysteries understood these things, but today mankind as a whole does not appreciate the subtler attributes of precious stones or metals, which are now used as ornaments, their real powers ignored and untapped.

Unfortunately, human society has become entangled in a web of intrigue and high finance involving politics, race and religion. Money has become a sinister ruling factor. I do not have to remind you that wars are as often fought because of the profits involved as for territorial or political reasons.

Governments set up monopoly commissions in a vain attempt to cope with such problems, yet very often they depend on income from the very institutions they seek to restrain.

From whichever angle you approach this subject, you will always come back to the matter of insecurity; seek still further and you will come to the inescapable conclusion that the only way to find real happiness is through inner peace and understanding entirely unrelated to money or possessions or gain.

Money is simply energy or fuel. Someone once described it as 'stored human energy', which is an extremely enlightened way of looking at it. The use of money, channelled constructively, is a manipulation of energy that can benefit mankind. It is not the use of money, but the abuse of money, that is evil.

To put it bluntly, money is yet another system (religion, politics and education are others) that sheer force of events will soon oblige you to re-think and re-create. When this happens, all these systems will be used for a higher purpose — to nourish mankind, not to control it.

18. Material Achievement

Some people measure their success in life purely in terms of their material achievements. Others sneer at material posses- sions, claiming that the only real achievements are mental, emotional and spiritual. What are your own views on the subject?

There is nothing unethical or wrong with material achieve- ment itself. It *can* lead to a sense of satisfaction and fulfilment, but just as often it carries misfortune and unhappiness in its wake, as it increases the danger of losing one's balance and perspective. All too often, having made his fortune, the rich man becomes obsessed with the pursuit of still more wealth, or retreats into idleness, complacency and self-indulgence. Also, it can be difficult for the rich man to know whether the people around him are his friends or whether they have just come along for the free ride.

Wealth is often considered immoral — especially by those who are unable to attain it themselves! I can assure you that well-earned gains such as financial success and possessions do not weigh the scales against you when you leave your physical body. The trouble lies not in the material gains themselves, but in the way you might lead your life after you have acquired them.

If by working harder than others or by using special skills you become wealthy, then it is for you to live your life as you see fit. If you use some of your money to help people less fortunate than yourself — in a way that helps them to evolve and not merely enables them to live off your riches — then you are doing something constructive.

How you handle success or wealth will naturally reflect your spiritual status. If a man who has amassed great wealth gives it away because he fears what might happen to him if he does not do so — do you really think he has done himself any good, or assisted his spiritual progress? So many people today are frightened and cannot accept themselves as they are. They can accept neither their own limitations nor their own possibilities, so they aspire to be what they are not, or what they wish other people to see — and they use money to achieve this.

Not until they throw aside this false identity and see themselves as they are, will a human society based on true values emerge.

Whether or not you have material success, my advice to you is: Do not try to be what you are not and cannot be; accept yourself as you are; live according to your *inner* self, endeavouring always to heighten and widen your perspectives, for in doing so you will grow in wisdom and understanding — which is the prime purpose of your being.

The time is coming when material possessions such as

those you prize today will be worthless. Money and its power will become things of the past, and mankind will achieve a spiritual maturity that will bring with it an entirely new set of values.

So you *do* have something to look forward to!

19. Politics

We gather that you don't think too highly of our politics!

Alas, the political systems of the world at present are either decadent, divisive, selfish and outmoded — or ruthless, repressive and soul-destroying. Where is the party or the policy today that is genuinely concerned with the welfare and fulfilment of the people as a whole? Even in Russia, where the system of government purports to be for the people, freedom of expression is a dangerous luxury.

Professional politicians are men and women whose only thought appears to be for the party, the status quo and themselves. This applies to all nations: I make no exceptions. Politics has become an intense and elaborate game of chess, in which each move is planned to undermine the opposition. Politicians, especially at election time, delude themselves into thinking that their sole interest is that of 'the people'. Particularly with the two-party system that exists in this country, an atmosphere of permanent antagonism and resentment exists: never are all sections of the public being helped.

So much more could be done to help people in many ways, but it is being sacrificed on the altar of party politics.

In time, however, an entirely new political concept will arise, and this will herald the beginning of another way of life altogether. It will eventually lead to a form of almost Atlantean government, in that it will make provision for the spiritual as well as the practical and material needs of the people.

This system will evolve gradually; to introduce it suddenly would be disastrous. It will have to be done in stages; the confidence of the public will have to be won, so that these things may be accomplished with the consent and co-operation of the people.

Eventually this type of administration will be adopted throughout the world, and will culminate in world government. The keystone of the matter will be tolerance, humility and compassion — especially tolerance of those with opposing beliefs.

There will be little of the destructive criticism and personal feuds that are daily heard in your council chambers today, where the main idea seems to be to score points, both political and personal, against the opposition.

"Oh come on, H-A," I hear the more cynical of you thinking to yourselves, "are you really serious? How could that happen, given human nature as it is?"

I am happy to say that, despite all the odds and probabilities, it *will* happen. It never could, of course, given your present attitudes and the systems that have sprung from them. But if you could only let go of your fears — all of you, everywhere, by an act of common will — there would be released a veritable tidal wave of positive energy and good-will; a nuclear chain reaction, as it were, of creativity and enlightenment. And it is towards this high goal that we must all begin to work — now.

There is no man, woman or child on Earth today who does not have a major contribution to make towards that distant yet approaching glory.

20. The Permissive Society

Is our so-called 'permissive society' a blessing or a curse?

I will, if I may, approach this from another altitude — much as an aircraft aligns itself with the runway before touching down.

Have you ever considered why it is that when you have an idea, you will often meet someone else to whom the same idea has just occurred? Ideas are impulses travelling along certain wavebands which can surface to the conscious from the subconscious mind — of one person, a group, or of many people simultaneously. This explains why tastes, fashions, trends and attitudes sometimes spread like wildfire: like minds have received the same impulse and, finding it compatible, respond to it.

With the arrival of the new age, more and more ideas are being beamed down to mankind, resulting in a general upsurge or awakening of consciousness. Recollections of races long forgotten, fragments of experiences undergone in previous lives, are flooding in. Also rising to the surface are memories of Atlantis at its height and the healing, science, art and knowledge that were achieved there.

This is an inheritance that is not to be dismissed or ignored. Rise, if you can, above the attitudes and thought-forms of the last two thousand years — during which the physical and emotional natures of man have been predominant — and on into the new age, whose chief purpose will be the mastery of your own minds.

And now we touch down on your question.

The paradox of man's development is that whenever there is an advancement in one area, a deterioration almost invariably occurs in another. The wise, bearing in mind the duality that characterises this world, will recognise and anticipate the phenomenon.

As you pass through each successive life here on Earth, you will gradually master the art of selection and discrimination. This process will strengthen your ability to remain steadfast to your choice — having examined various alternatives before arriving at your decision. Temptations and distractions there will always be, but as your sense of 'what is right for me' continues to develop, you will no longer care if those around you, indulging themselves in various ways, shout, "Coward! You don't know what you're missing!"

That is just the point: by this time you *will* know what you are missing — and you'll be only too glad to miss it! Cries of derision will no longer affect you, nor will you feel any great sense of loss or isolation, because by this time you will be in contact with your higher self which will already be offering you vistas and perspectives, adventures and experiences compared with which the trends and excitements of the day are very small fry indeed!

When we look at the world today we are most encouraged to see how many people are bringing back some of the wisdom of previous ages. But as the good is recalled, so is the destructive element and, under the guise of 'freedom', so-called, this destructive element slips in and becomes firmly entrenched. Permissiveness is the very thing that will set off alarm bells in the mind of everyone who remembers how and why so many past civilisations collapsed.

"Ah yes," I hear you say, "but after all the cruelties and the repression of ordinary people throughout history by one tyranny or dictatorship after another, who wouldn't fling his hat in the air to welcome a period of comparative freedom of choice?" And to this I must reply that my hat is up there among yours!

Inexorably, as humanity awakes to its identity and its rights, such obstructions as religious and political persecution, brainwashing and the forces that condition and dehumanise will all be cast aside.

Yet in one respect the pendulum has already swung too far, and certain unscrupulous men are taking advantage of it: immature people of all ages are now under tremendous pressure to be 'with it', to go along with the mob; to blow their minds and destroy their health with drugs obtained from deluded profiteers and even governmental bodies,* who claim that what they are peddling is proof of an 'enlightened' and 'emancipated' age.

---

*H-A is referring to parts of the world where governments have legalised the use of hard drugs, such as heroin, for registered addicts.

I hardly have to remind anyone who has the slightest acquaintance with the law of Karma that to engage in the deliberate debasement of other human beings for profit can only heap retribution sooner or later on these unhappy perpetrators.

There are many imbalances today: it is a moment of polarity and extremes. But the brighter it gets, the deeper will the surrounding darkness seem to be. It is time to light the light within yourself — to stand up and be counted. More and more enlightened souls are incarnating now, both to experience and to assist at this unique planetary Moment — the birth of a new age.

21. There *is* no Death

Death is a subject most people prefer not to talk about, and funerals are positively dreaded. The media haven't helped — all they ever seem to do is relate the subject to horror and hauntings and ghouls and graves giving up their dead . . .

There *is* no death. Only transformation. Hold on to this truth, and your perspective on everything will change.

Does a tree die in winter? Everything about its appearance suggests that it does — but we know that it has simply withdrawn into itself and is quietly preparing to re-emerge into the coming year. The entire process is no more than a breathing in and a breathing out again. This occurs in all things, from the smallest particles to the Universe itself.

As man has become ever more deeply embedded in matter, he has gradually lost sight of who he really is, where he comes from, why he visits Earth and where he goes when each phase of this adventure is over.

Corrupt men and regimes have always sought to control the people in their power — and what better way to achieve this than by using fear? Fear of living, fear of poverty, fear of war, fear of reprisals, fear of death and nothingness. Result? Untold generations have lost heart, lost the will to question and explore, resigned themselves to monotony and debt and servitude; and, believing they have nothing to look forward to, have become as clay in the hands of ruthless men who have sent them to work and to war, for centuries on end.

This has been a worldwide manipulation of your minds, your lives, your souls.

If I can throw a little light on this transition you now call death — but which I recommend that you call 'rebirth' or 'reawakening' — it might serve to reassure you.

As some of you already know, the physical body is discarded by the spirit at the appointed time, and this applies whatever age the body has attained: many spirits decide to incarnate for only a short period.

Generally speaking, when a person has just "died" the spirit has the entire record of its recent Earth life still with it and consequently might not realise what has happened. Whenever possible, it will be helped by those who have already passed over to negotiate the next step more easily.

It takes anything from a few minutes to a few days before the spirit finally leaves the body and the silver cord is dissolved; this is often done by those who have come to help. According to the evolution and understanding of the spirit passing over, these helpers may need to enlighten it as to what has happened — and this is often necessary because of the state of mind in which the person dies.

If a body has met an abrupt end such as in war, murder or in an accident, the spirit needs immediate help as it may have been catapulted away from its physical shell at high speed. Such a spirit, confused and disorientated, needs more time than most to recover. And the longer it has, the better. If it reincarnates too quickly, some form of mutation will probably result, either physical, mental or even spiritual. Many spirits remain earthbound, unaware of the death of their physical bodies. They are helped by other discarnate beings and occasionally by those who are incarnate, to realise what has happened and then they pass on their way.

Far from being a tragic event, death is a step forward in any spirit's development and something to celebrate rather than mourn. How much better it would be for all concerned if you were able to look at it this way, instead of regarding death as a personal loss — without giving any thought to the release and upliftment that the spirit has probably undergone in passing.

It is understandable that the death of a friend or close relative will cause sadness, but the moment you realise that it is the right time for the spirit in question to pass on — maybe bringing a period of great suffering and pain to an end — and that it is even now progressing still further, you will be able to resume your own life not only without grief or fear, but even with a sense of reassurance. Unfortunately, many of you dwell morbidly on the past, impeding your own progress and also — which is almost worse — holding back your loved ones by your possessive thoughts.

The time is long overdue that man should begin to regard death in its proper perspective: as no more than a falling asleep and a reawakening.

What an appalling waste it would be if death really *were*

the end of a human spirit! Think of all that effort and experience and creativity being thrown away. . . But Nature abhors waste as much as it abhors a vacuum, so nothing is thrown away, everything is recycled.

Take heart: when you discard your physical body — as you would an old overcoat — the inner 'you' returns to the higher planes with all its recent knowledge, experience and skills, its loves and friendships intact.

You *can* take it with you!

In what light do you see the death of a small child or baby?

Although it is very distressing for the parents, there are many reasons why a spirit might choose to enter a body for only a short period of time.

It may, this time round, need only that short period of attunement with physical life; and it may also be helping the evolution of its parents through the understanding they gain from its early demise.

That short life may be a 'trial run' in preparation for a forthcoming incarnation, even to the same parents. The possibilities are infinite.

Remember, from the moment of conception a spirit is experiencing and learning from its experience.

OUR ORIGINS

22. Life before 'Birth' and after 'Death'

Many people who have passed over describe their new surroundings as 'the Summerland'. Is this place real or imaginary?'

When your spirit, having recently left your body at 'death', first adjusts itself to its surroundings, a whole new existence opens up before it. And remember, although free now of physical limitations, it is still limited by its own experience and understanding.

So, a spirit finds itself free of the constraints of a physical body. What happens? Because it is sheer thought, it can conjure all kinds of situations just by thinking them — a waking dream without interruptions, limited only by its creator's own imaginative powers. This is why, when you receive messages from this level — which is close to the Earth plane — they tend to sound like descriptions of an idealised garden of paradise, equipped to gratify the wildest fantasies. Yet this state is only one of many levels or dimensions that lie before every developing soul.

What about the people who don't believe in life after death? What happens when they pass over?

They will probably remain earthbound for a time. This happens because they refuse to accept that they no longer have a physical body and so create one by their own thought power. There are many spirits wandering through the ether today who imagine themselves to be incarnate when they are not. This not only holds back their own development but can cause inconvenience to others; however, they are usually helped sooner or later to realise their mistake and go on their way.*

In the case of a person who dies slowly, knowing he is dying and expecting nothing when he does so, the spirit may remain in a state of coma after leaving the body — because it is expecting nothing it will receive nothing until other spirits manage to reawaken it.

A widespread failure to accept life before and after death is one of the factors now holding back the evolution of the entire human race and of the planet itself, as it is causing a number of premature, almost 'blind' incarnations: all too many spirits coming back into physical bodies without fully understanding why they have done so.

---

*A sensitive in Los Angeles has reported that for several days after his death, Humphrey Bogart wandered about his home, distressed that his wife, Lauren Bacall, kept ignoring him. Spirit friends had trouble persuading Bogart that he had died, and that his widow could no longer see or hear him. Eventually, the reluctant Bogart was convinced and his new friends helped him on his way.

Maybe it's the fear of some sort of reckoning or Day of Judgement that makes people fear death?

I do not particularly enjoy shattering anyone's pet illusions, but I must emphasise that this 'Day of Judgement' *is* an illusion. God does not judge. In fact, the more evolved a spirit is, the less inclined is it to judge. Only humans in their foolishness try to pass judgement on others.

When your present life ends, *you* will assess it yourself and, because you will no longer be limited by physical dimensions, your vision will be wider than when you were in the body. You will see yourself for what you really are and for what you might have been and, believe me, you will be a far harsher judge of yourself than God, if He judged, would ever be.

This self-knowledge or self-realisation of a spirit newly returned to the inner planes is in itself a form of initiation, and for many it can be a temporary state of purgation.

Does the hell described by certain religions really exist?

My answer is that it is a mental state and exists for those who wish to make it exist. Many spirits choose to torture themselves to atone for what they have done. It is possible, however, to rise above this self-punishment by achieving a complete understanding of the error made, and by totally forgiving oneself and any other being involved.

What of ghosts?

When you speak of ghosts you are principally referring to two types of spirit. First, those that have left their Earth bodies but, out of ignorance, guilt, atonement or a desire for no more than the physical plane has to offer, cannot leave their Earth surroundings; and secondly, elementary spirits in a stage of pre-human existence. The latter should not be confused with the spirits of the elements, which belong to another form of evolution altogether.

Other ghostly apparitions can be caused by conscious astral projection: you imagine yourself somewhere else and a sensitive person 'sees' you there; or by self-induced hallucination. And as you well know, a person who has just died can appear to a loved one sensitive enough to see him or her.

23. Heaven's Above

Could you describe the spirit planes?

When a spirit first leaves the body it is often 'lost' for a while. It is no longer hampered by a physical vehicle, one that perhaps caused it much suffering. It is like being suddenly released from prison after many years 'inside'. The spirit may be met by friends who will explain what has happened or, if it is undeveloped, it may not realise that it has passed over and will continue to live as it did while incarnate.

Some spirits rest for a while after passing as they are still feeling the strain of being cooped up for so long, or maybe the after-effects of whatever disabilities their discarded bodies suffered. They then move on after a period of rest and healing either to gladness or to sorrow. Often they rejoice at first, then they remember the things they have left undone or mishandled and ask themselves if they are fit and ready to proceed. Perhaps the spirit will immediately decide to serve another term on Earth and, if it makes this decision, it will then select a body that is to undergo the type of experience it needs and enter it at conception.

When you die, there are helpers who will assist your spirit in its transition to the first of the spirit planes. There are six major spirit planes between physical existence and the Ultimate but, as Earth is sometimes counted as a plane of experience, many people number them as seven: Earth is designated as the first plane, the nearest spirit world to Earth as the second, and the Ultimate as the seventh.

These broad divisions give a rough indication of life beyond the physical. They are not, of course, separate areas of existence but frequencies or states of being interpenetrating each other. Dense matter is one of the lowest forms of vibration and the grosser the substance the lower its frequency. Fast-moving rays such as X-rays and gamma rays pass effortlessly through matter without necessarily changing its composition, in much the same way as a 'ghost' passes through a wall or door.

When a spirit feels that it can go ahead and experience further, its new awareness will raise it to the next plane. As the wisdom of the spirit grows, its vibration or frequency becomes finer and higher until, eventually, it is so fine that it achieves a state of complete harmony with the Ultimate itself.

Let us now take a brief look at the six spirit planes — bearing in mind the total inadequacy of words to describe them:

Second Plane
This is the plane often referred to as the 'Summerland'. Here a spirit is at liberty to re-create Earth conditions as it saw them in

its physical body, or to create fantasies to gratify repressed yearnings. But in these instances it is merely conjuring what it wishes to see. A spirit can remain in this state for any length of time, according to its desire to progress. The spirits of people who have been very materially minded or self-indulgent or immature will often elect to stay here for a long time. They may also reincarnate again and again with little forethought or wisdom, into similar bodies undergoing similar experiences. Eventually they reach a stage of understanding that enables them to move on. They may then choose a life that gives them an opportunity to learn of values that are other than purely material or self-indulgent, and in time this more enlightened thought state will enable them, when next discarnate, to ascend to the third plane.

Those who have led violent or destructive lives often pass over full of bitterness and resentment and, because they still harbour evil thoughts, they attract others in the spirit world of a like mind. They all indulge their fantasies together, experiencing a self-imposed state of hell. This is, as I have said, only a mental state. These spirits dwell there until they realise that they can gain no further satisfaction from such activities. God is all-merciful and condemns no-one: when a spirit has learnt tolerance and humility or acknowledges its own shortcomings, it is given another chance to redeem itself.

Third Plane

As soon as a newcomer arrives on the third plane, many others will come to assist it. It will learn something of the physical Universe, the cosmos and the Ultimate. It is then faced with a choice as it realises its experience is still incomplete. It may decide that it doesn't need another incarnation for a while, but will gain experience by helping someone on Earth.

A spirit that decides to help in some capacity from the inner planes does not necessarily choose the vocation of its last incarnation. For instance, if a person was a musician three incarnations ago, that knowledge would not be lost to him, but he may feel only now that his musical experience can be put to good use, so he resolves to help someone in this capacity.

The number of people a spirit can guide is not limited: it still has free will and can progress as it wishes. A spirit may guide only one person, or several. Eventually the time comes when its knowledge and wisdom uplift it to the next plane.

Fourth Plane

When a being has ascended through the second and third planes, it may feel that it has no further need for physical incarnation. What are its discoveries when it reaches the fourth plane?

This is the realm of colour, and here you will find yourself among indescribable hues which make even those on Earth seem inadequate — if only because they are of another dimension altogether.

How do these colours come to be, and what is their purpose? They are the result of a fusion of spirit and experience at different levels within the fourth plane. Similarly, your every feeling, thought and action as a human being can be allied to colour. Within the fourth plane the spirit begins by exploring the lower or darker octaves of colour and graduates to the higher or lighter octaves.

Upon entering the first colour you will find a rich and varied experience awaiting you; you will be engulfed in a dimension of music that beggars description. On the waves of this multidimensional sound you will be guided to various planets and celestial bodies where you have perhaps undergone earlier physical experience. Possibly your function at this stage will be to help an incarnate person or group of individuals in a special task; or you might join a group of spirits that is teaching others from the second and third planes.

As the wisdom and experience of the spirit grows, its vibration becomes finer. And so it ascends, metaphorically speaking. Although at this stage it is still within the confines of the fourth plane, it now enters an entirely different dimension where the colour is even lighter and of a new brilliance, and the quality of sound indescribable. This is followed by a period of 'evolutionary meditation', a process whereby a spirit ascends by gradually assimilating an awareness of even higher thought around it. It will then, after certain tests and initiations, pass through another series of dimensions each a little lighter in vibration that the previous one until, after this natural process of becoming finer and wiser, it enters the fifth plane, a world of pure spirit and an infinity unto itself.

Here I must make one thing very clear: these spheres above and beyond the fourth plane are not replicas or affinities of any physical world, nor are they in any way concerned with physical planets, solar systems or galaxies of any sort. Anyone allowed a glimpse of these realms would only gain the vaguest impression of their nature and immensity, an impression that it would be virtually impossible to translate into Earth terms.

Fifth Plane

This realm is one of illumination where the spirit is uplifted by the beauty, the wonder and the wisdom of Creation. Here the spirit learns to be a creator in its own right. It is a preparation for the sixth plane, the highest before the Ultimate. It is a region where the spirit rests and ponders its previous learning and reviews its evolution so far. It is called by some the plane of Light.

Sixth Plane

The sixth plane is one of inexpressible majesty and magnitude. The exalted beings who guide planets are usually from this plane and would probably be known to you as Seraphim and Cherubim or ascended Masters, depending on the sphere of evolution to which they belong. Here the spirit broadens its vision to encompass all worlds and all planes, and adjusts itself to the total and awesome realisation of its final step to the Ultimate — a oneness with God.

Seventh Plane

Everything is in God's imagination. Without it, nothing would exist. When a spirit finally returns to the Ultimate, it retains a certain amount of its individuality and yet is in complete harmony with all other thought.

The Godhead is an expanding force and each returning spirit, having achieved that degree of fineness, breadth of thought and understanding, adds to the infinity of experience within the Godhead. The spirit itself continues to expand in complete harmony and oneness until it merges into such greatness that there are no words to describe it.

Many people think that the various spirit worlds stretch between the Earth and some remote, unattainable point which they consider to be God. This is not so: all spirit worlds interweave, so that *within you and your home* all are present, from the densest to the Godhead itself.

It would be much more accurate to think in terms of spiritual filters: as a spirit advances it becomes finer and naturally 'percolates' through to a higher vibration. The Godhead, being finest of all, pervades all!

Finally, I would like to re-emphasise that although we are classifying the Earth, then five spirit planes and finally the Godhead as the seventh or Ultimate plane, these are only broad divisions to help you visualise existence beyond the physical. One could as well divide these planes into forty-nine, a thousand or indeed an infinite number, as each provides a wealth of experience in itself. Such are the 'many mansions' awaiting every explorer in this infinite cosmos.

24. Pre-Human Existence

You say that spirits leave the Godhead as individual thoughts and eventually decide which lifestream or kingdom they will experience through. Is there some halfway stage or level they go to before making their final choice?

Yes. There is a realm below that of human existence known as the plane of decision. When a spirit first leaves the Ultimate it goes to this plane and there it undergoes a series of experiences until it chooses to enter either the human, animal, vegetable, mineral or some other kingdom.

Let us leave aside the animal kingdom for a moment and look at the spirit emerging from the plane of decision to experience human life. It may first enter into an intermediate stage while trying to find its own level; such spirits occasionally manifest as an elementary spirit or poltergeist. Sooner or later, however, the need to incarnate will dawn on it and it will enter a human body.

Spirits that have chosen to experience through animal evolution do not normally switch over to human existence.

There are exceptions to this rule but they are extremely rare, as each evolutionary group follows its own stream of experience quite independently.

You will have noticed that many human beings are young in understanding and comparatively unthinking, whereas others are mature, thoughtful and compassionate. This is because the former are comparatively new to human existence — maybe incarnating for the first time — and the latter have progressed further along the path and have gained more wisdom. Ideally, these more advanced souls will offer compassionate leadership and guidance to the many young souls who outnumber them — and these younger souls will recognise and accept such leadership gladly, without resentment.

25. Twin Souls and Group Souls

When a spirit leaves the Ultimate and 'descends' to the lower planes to gather experience, it meets up with what is known as a 'group soul'. This is a collection of spirits that have banded together because they left the Godhead together and have decided that, broadly speaking, they would like to experience together. As the group soul evolves, so do the people within it. They grow wiser and more mature and complement each other, building and achieving great collective powers.

The ultimate form of experience, however, is not a group experience but the development of every single spirit as a wholly unique being. Experiencing within the group soul is very beneficial and reassuring up to a point, but it can be restricting to individual growth. Discovering who you really are and what you can achieve is your ultimate challenge.

There are no such things as 'twin souls' as you may have heard it expressed. Two similar spirits can frequently incarnate together and, because of this, influence each other. They often enter the bodies of twins, hence the special affinity.

When two spirits achieve great love and harmony in an Earth life, such as may exist between man and wife, they are not necessarily destined to repeat the process in a subsequent life. They may choose to help each other in some other way — perhaps as brother and sister or as close friends of either sex, because to repeat a harmonious experience in a similar relationship would not necessarily further their evolution but might even stagnate it. The love between spirits is purely spiritual and is a true harmony, transcending physical senses and even emotions.

26. Do Humans Evolve from Animals?

The evolution of animals is entirely different from that of human beings. When a spirit is on the plane of decision it decides which evolutionary stream to enter. A spirit that chooses to experience as an animal does *not* subsequently enter a human body — except in rare circumstances — but progresses through the animal kingdom to the spirit planes, ascending in much the same way as the spirit of a human.

Although all spirits are as one in the sense that they are the offspring or 'thoughts' of the Ultimate, the experiences they elect to undergo give them that individuality which distinguishes, for instance, the spirit of a cat from that of a plant or a human being. They are like branches of a tree, the tree of life itself, each branch representing a different form of evolution and contributing its share of experience to the whole.

When we begin to examine various life forms, particularly those of animals and human beings, we have to bear two separate factors in mind. First, there is the physical aspect: human beings and animals have undoubtedly evolved from the same life cells; the brain capacity of an animal is smaller than that of a human being and its type of experience is on the whole very much more limited. But when we come to the question of *spirit* evolution it is a quite different story.

In all physical expression there is the fusion of two types of evolution — the spiritual and the physical. The spirit expresses through the medium of physical matter. When, at 'death', the body disintegrates and returns to its component elements, the spirit, being eternal, continues to develop by means of further incarnations in the physical world, interspersed with periods of rest and learning on the inner planes. Eventually it ceases to need physical expression altogether and it then moves on permanently to other realms.

Physically, then, men and animals did originate in the same life cell but, from the spirit point of view, mankind is a form of evolution entire unto itself. What was the 'missing link', you may ask, and when did the transitional stage occur?

The true emergence of man on Earth dates from the moment when a new type of spirit entered the bodies of advanced apes, influencing the growth and size of their physical brains, causing them gradually to develop the faculties of discernment and creativity. Early progress was slow but, as bodily development progressed and brain capacity increased, a more evolved human spirit was able to take over. And so it went on until the pattern of *homo sapiens* slowly emerged, branching off from the mainstream of animal evolution.

Man does not like to consider that animal evolution, from the spiritual point of view, is as elevated as his own; but I can assure you that a cat that walks in on a gathering of people could have a more advanced spirit than any of those present. And this is no insult to anyone!

All the time you are undergoing physical experience in various incarnations, your spirit is growing in understanding. Whether a spirit chooses to grow through the cat family, the horse family or the human family, there comes a time when it has no further need of physical experience — its spirit has become finer, lighter and wiser as it climbs further up the ladder of spiritual evolution. You will appreciate that when this occurs it has not reached the Godhead by any means; in fact it still has a long way to go.

Whereas animal evolution is quite different from human, these two kingdoms exist side by side for a purpose: to serve and learn from each other. Before you condemn the occasional 'rogue' animal that preys on man, consider the wholesale slaughter of animals by humans — a slaughter that ranges from mindless 'sport' to murder on the grand scale.

All such karmic debts must, in time, be paid.

27. Animal Evolution

Do animals change their species during successive incarnations? Do they have free will? And are some animals more evolved than others?

I should like to answer the last question first by saying that some species do enjoy a lower state of consciousness than others. The fish is an example of this, its conscious expression being far more restricted than that of a cow or a pig. Even so, within the fish family there are widely differing levels of evolution. Take the dolphin: its intelligence has in recent times startled marine biologists and the general public alike, fully justifying the claim that the dolphin, of all other creatures on earth, has an intelligence comparable with that of man himself.

Animals do not change their type. For example, a spirit that chooses to experience as a cat would not return after two or three incarnations as a horse or dog, but would explore the many branches of the cat family. Your cat may once have been a lion or a tiger; if you look at it closely you will probably observe a likeness to one particular branch of the big cat family. The same applies to the domestic dog, whose spirit may have started as a wolf or jackal before becoming the docile creature who sleeps so contentedly by your fireside. The number of incarnations an animal may have can no more be assessed than the number a human undergoes; there are no hard and fast rules, as each spirit advances at its own speed.

Do animals have free will? Yes, to a point, but not in the same way as you know it. The free will of an animal is limited to the choice its spirit makes when it is discarnate. As soon as it enters the chosen body it is subject to the natural conditions and limitations of that body and is obliged to accept them.

The spirits of animals can appear from the inner planes in exactly the same way as human spirits, and clairvoyants often see them. Your deceased pet may stay with you for a long time to try to help you from the inner planes. Some animals, especially cats, are excellent guards against lower astral influences; ancient civilisations knew of these powers and made use of them, hence the 'familiar' of the witch or wizard. Animals that have become very attached to their human friends may even follow them through the spirit and material worlds. You may have known your pet on several previous occasions.

The cat and the dog are approximately at the same stage of development, although they express themselves differently. The cat embodies the passive, receptive instinct and the dog, the active. Some animals in each species are more evolved than their fellows, just as certain men and women are. You can no more make rules about the evolutionary status of your pets than you can about your friends and fellow men.

One factor should not be overlooked: each animal is an individual, just as you are. They have their own traits of personality and character and will serve man in the way best suited. Treat your animals gently yet firmly, try to understand them. To feed them and turn them out occasionally is not enough; nor is excessive pampering and overfeeding to be encouraged. They need to give and receive affection, as do humans; and although they cannot answer you verbally or earn money for their keep, they can give you sympathy and a loyalty and affection you sometimes find difficult to achieve with your fellow human beings.

Long ago all animals were the friends of man and did not attack him, but in those days man knew how to communicate with his animal brothers and sisters in a way that has been lost during centuries of cruelty and callousness. We can, however, look forward to the future when such a relationship will be restored and all forms of evolution on Earth will be reconciled once again.

For the man who believes himself to be spiritually superior to his animal cousins, the time of reckoning will come when he will meet them face to face in the world of spirit, unfettered by the limitations and advantages of brain and body. There are shocks in store for many people: God has many faces and many names and within the infinity of the Godhead are *all* forms of existence.

28. Body and Spirit — Do they Evolve Together?

As you know, the spirit is the 'I', the essential you, that spark which gives you being and causes you to initiate thoughts and ideas. It began as a thought created by the Godhead and entered a Universe of infinite experience as pure, untried thought, an embryo without depth, vision, understanding nor wisdom yet, like a seed, containing infinite potential.

Every moment of your life you are learning. Every action, every decision that you make is helping to mould you. Life consists of a series of challenges that have to be met; all the time you are having to make decisions that affect your entire future. Some of these decisions are simple, being part of everyday routine; others are more difficult because they involve other people around you, those dear to you, those with whom you work. The challenge is to meet each situation as it arises; deal with it, cope with it. You cannot expect to make the right decision every time but to make one, even if it is wrong, is often better than making none at all. In any event, the choices you make and the habits you acquire now are shaping not only the rest of your present incarnation but also your future lives.

And so we come to one of the most interesting paradoxes of physical incarnation. Although your spirit has free will and contains the sum total of all its past lives and pre-human experiences, in a physical body its options are somewhat curtailed by the limitations of genetics, environment and the actions of other human beings around it. So one of the first things an incarnating spirit has to do is to come to terms with its physical shell. This is not always easy and will depend upon the relationship between the ego and its vehicle.

Many of you wonder why you do not recall your past lives because you feel it could be helpful to your present incarnation. Although it may seem strange to you, it is for the best that the vast majority of people are not burdened with memories of their successes, failures and traumas of past lives, but are free to concentrate on making what they can of their present life. You do, after all, retain the wisdom you have gained from *all* previous experience and the particular challenges you face in your present life will, in themselves, reveal the lessons you set yourself prior to conception. (There are, of course, exceptions where awareness of an event in a past life can help in therapy.)

Wisdom is not in any way bound by intelligence. A person can have a brain of quite limited capacity yet can house a spirit of great wisdom and beauty. One of the deepest traps you can fall into is to think that intellect and academic prowess imply evolution and wisdom. True wisdom is simplicity and it takes a very special person to be able to view a complex situation in a simple way. The ability not to become enmeshed in too much detail or day-to-day complications is the hallmark of wisdom.

Physical appearance to a certain extent reflects the state of the spirit. A highly evolved spirit would not incarnate into the body of, say, Neanderthal man, through which it could not express itself. This does not mean that people of handsome appearance are necessarily evolved, for it is not good looks but wisdom and character that indicate inner worth. Nevertheless, spiritual and physical evolution do run side by side and a serious lack of this evolutionary alignment can cause genetic deformities. The balanced spirit can cope, but those less balanced cannot, and it is they who are most likely to be affected by negative and destructive influences around them.

To sum up: body and spirit are separate forms of evolution although, when integrated into physical life, they evolve together as a whole unit, each influencing the other. Making the most of your incarnation is a growing process of coming to terms with all aspects of yourself, learning to accept yourself as you are, no more and no less. It is finding your own harmony, your inner melody which will enable you to develop to the full all the positive and loving aspects of your individual character.

29. Help from Unseen Friends

Most people are quite unaware of the help they receive from the spirit planes in the form of inspiration, ideas, protection, guidance and the many so-called coincidences that have a powerful effect on their lives.

There are many ways in which discarnate beings are able to help those who are incarnate, to their mutual benefit. Certain spirits act as guides, helping one particular person throughout his or her Earth life. They are sometimes referred to as 'door-keepers' or guardian angels and their service is not unrewarded: they too learn from the experience in many instances. In the case of a medium or sensitive they also stand guard when psychic work is being done and protect their charges from less evolved spirits that might try to interfere.

It is possible to change one's guardian or guide during a lifetime, but this usually only happens when the course of a person's life has been radically altered so that he or she can undertake specific work in a new direction.

Then there are those spirits who may wish to assist someone for a specific purpose, so they attach themselves to that person for a particular period. For example, a guide might give specialised help to someone studying for an examination or researching a project, or to a writer, designer, musician, scientist, actor, engineer, teacher or politician at some key moment. Once sufficient help has been given the spirit will withdraw and turn to others in a similar situation.

Guides that give practical assistance usually come from the third plane, but of course this is not always the case. Guidance of a spiritual or esoteric nature, for example, is often given by those who have evolved to the fourth plane.

At one time or another, most human beings are helped not only by their principal guide or guardian, but by loved ones, specialists and other spirits with whom they may have established a vital connection on some previous occasion.

What would the human race do, without this hidden network of helpers, this unseen influence? The thought does not bear thinking about! Suffice it to say, the Universe is very much more integrated than you imagine it to be. You are not isolated. You are a unique part of an infinite wholeness.

30. How you Choose a Body for Reincarnation

When a spirit first leaves the Godhead it is virtually without experience, knowledge or wisdom. It is like an unopened pod. Then gradually it begins to unfold. One of its first experiences is deciding which lifestream to enter. If it chooses physical evolution it may select the mineral kingdom and attach itself to some form of rock, soil or marine life, or perhaps it may choose vegetation, the animal kingdom or *homo sapiens*.

If it chooses the elements, however, it will be operating on a very much stronger type of vibration than that of man. The elemental frequency is perceptibly 'sharper' than your own.

Entering into an Earth body is not a form of spiritual roulette, nor is it decided by sticking a pin in a map: you first incarnate as part of a group soul and you will soon meet up with other members of your group already there waiting to help you. You begin to experience Earth life — family, surroundings, friends, challenges — and your spirit shares in these adventures, learning from your successes and your failures. Some lessons you learn quickly, such as not to put your hand into a fire or jump from a high window or step in front of moving traffic. Others are more subtle and complex, and you may make the same mistake again and again — or learn the first time. This is evolution.

Many sects and regimes impose a rigid dogma on their followers, who accept these restrictions gladly because they provide psychological security and an excuse to evade their own responsibilities. They do not have to think for themselves because someone has presented them with a set of rules and ideas with each detail neatly ticked and filed in the right place. All very well and good — but how limiting! All you will learn from this will be somebody else's concepts.

The simplest way to advance spiritually is to be open-minded, to think for yourself, to be prepared to learn from and to serve others. Your spirit will choose a body appropriate to the experiences it needs.

Before you entered your present body you made your choice with the help of other guides and friends from your group. You were able to see the broad outline of the life that lay ahead of you, the overall pattern it presented, the karma. The view from the inner planes is very rarely detailed in the way that incarnate people view the minor facets of their lives.

When spirits are young they tend, as I have said, to incarnate with a group, following the general impulse that can be generated by a band of spirits moving together along their chosen path. Young souls do not like to separate from the group and will gravitate back to it should they happen to incarnate among those of another type. Evidence of the group soul can be seen anywhere in life that people act together *en masse* rather than as individuals.

But as a spirit grows in stature it individualises and eventually leaves its group to branch out on its own. This can be painful as it means leaving the security of the group and perhaps the religion to which the group originally affiliated itself. In such an incarnation you will have to accept new ideas and carry out much soul-searching. You may choose to work with smaller groups for specific purposes, together with other spirits with whom you are in sympathy.

You may have wondered whether selecting this or that life for yourself amounts to predestination once you are incarnate. Your free will ensures that it does not: you can alter course whenever you wish. Remember, Fate is *not* a stranger waiting round the corner to ambush you — it is the outcome of how you handle your life.

If somebody predicts what is going to happen to you next week, it is not because your future is already preordained but because they have seen the results of certain decisions you are probably going to make. This is why some people, after visiting clairvoyants, change their lives by making decisions to fit what they have just been told. Depending on the accuracy and significance of the seer's visions, this can either be a good thing (a mishap might be averted) or a bad (a challenge or responsibility might be sidestepped).

Let us take an example, whom we shall call John. At the age of twenty-three John meets a girl, but he does not feel ready to marry although it is part of his karma to do so at that time. Ten years later he meets someone else and marries her. John has altered his karma and, when he finishes that life, his spirit will look back and see that when it entered that body it had planned to travel past certain milestones. It sees that John did not reach all the intended milestones but achieved certain other results that had not been planned. It can see how he handled the problems of that incarnation and may be pleased with what it has gained from the experience.

On the other hand, it may be filled with remorse. Perhaps John lived during a war and committed atrocities. His spirit, no longer fettered by the emotions and constraints of a physical body, will probably feel badly about this — and may even create its own temporary hell. As I have explained elsewhere, hell is not a mythical state of fire and brimstone, it is a state of mind that spirits create for themselves when they are faced with their destructiveness and cruelty during their recent Earth life. And a region where those who relish evil act out their degraded fantasies.

Each one of you is responsible to yourself: it is *your* conscience you will have to face when you leave your physical existence. I am convinced that if everyone knew this it would make a great difference to their outlook.

When John's spirit has sorted out all the whys and wherefores of its recent incarnation, gone through its purgation and emerged from it, it may feel that it still has a lot to learn from physical life. It will understand the lessons it has learnt, will acknowledge those it has failed and will recognise the type of experience it now needs to complement that already undergone.

John's spirit does not arrive at these decisions on its own: there are others around to help and advise. And it is not forced to take on another life even though the idea may be suggested by wiser souls. The final decision will arise out of its own mental processes.

If it does decide to reincarnate, John's spirit, again with the help of others more experienced, will have the opportunity to choose the type of life that will be most appropriate. Being in a state of pure thought, with no physical body or emotions to make it want to take the easiest path, it may well choose a difficult life, either to atone for past misdeeds or purely as a means of learning. It may choose parents that give it a difficult childhood. It may take on the role of a cripple or someone fraught with mental or emotional problems. It will be shown the milestones of this life and what they represent. Hence the importance of *accepting* your life, of coming to terms with it, however arduous and painful it may seem, because *your own inner self has chosen it and it is your own record you will have to review when you leave it.*

John's spirit will continue to incarnate into a succession of physical bodies until it has mastered the lessons to be learned from material existence. It is then ready to enter other realms.

You are probably familiar with the old saying that there are many paths to the centre of a city. Take whichever path you will: it is your own individual one and let me assure you that no-one else will ever tread it — although many others may intersect it or even join it for a whole.

Life is not something to fear or to dread, it is an adventure to enjoy, to make the most of, because it is enabling your spirit to meet challenges, to temper its free will, to rise above limitations and to grow in wisdom and vision.

Take social and personal limitations — you may live in a tribe in the Andes or a community in Vietnam, you may live in New York, Iceland or Central Africa. But wherever you live, your life is influenced by prevailing conditions. Are you poor? Are you wealthy? Are you fit or is your body ailing? Are your parents kind and helpful? How do your neighbours treat you? How many real friends do you have? Do you find it easy to give to others — not in the monetary or material sense, but of yourself? Do you enjoy extending warmth and sympathy to others or do you find it hard to communicate? Do you want to withdraw and isolate yourself or do you want to live surrounded by other people? Do you have a keen intellect or not?

Life is full of conditioning factors and these are the things that prevent you from having complete free will while incarnate. On the other hand, your spirit learns much through accepting limitations and finding its own freedom within those conditions. But there is still plenty of scope — in free countries at least — because if you do not want to live where you are, you can move on; if you do not like your job you can find another. If you are a shy, retiring person and you make positive efforts to overcome this defect, you will be rewarded when you extend warmth and friendship to others.

All outer conditions and limitations need to be accepted because, on a higher level, you have almost certainly chosen them for yourself. And, if you really understand them, you will be very close to finding the reason for your present life — the lessons you have come to learn.

Everything you do and think now is shaping your future. After all, is not your life one series of 'nows'? What has gone before must influence what you are doing now; learn from it and try not to repeat mistakes. One mistake is to live in the past, some period when, in retrospect, all seemed very rosy. Equally important is not to create castles in the air, expecting improbable things to happen which will solve all present difficulties. Consider the future, yes, but always with an open mind, prepared to adapt yourself to the unexpected turns life takes. And never lose the ability to laugh. Laughter and humour are two of the most healing and disarming weapons you will ever possess.

When your spirit enters a physical body it brings with it all the experience you have ever had in the past, and this is stored in the subconscious mind. On occasion, when the going gets tough or the opposition intensifies, you might be tempted to say, either in self-justification or self-pity, 'Don't blame me — I didn't *ask* to be born. . .'

But you did, my friend, you did!

OUR PLANET

31. The Beginning of Earth

How was the Earth born?

To put it scientifically — and simply — the Universe is composed of energy manifesting at different frequencies. It is by means of these various speeds or octaves of vibration that different substances come into being. The spirit is a very fine thought, a very fine substance if you prefer, so fine that you cannot see it with your physical eyes; whereas you can see anything physical, such as other human beings, because they are vibrating at the same rate as yourself. One discarnate spirit can recognise another just as you can recognise your friends because, when you have two spirits evolving together on, say, the third plane, they are both moving — vibrating — at the same rate. Although they would be much too fine for you to see they are, of course, quite real to each other: to them, the world of spirit *is* reality.

As you read this you are aware of yourself, you can feel that you are here, solid and foursquare and real. You can also look at your neighbour, you are able to see and touch him or her, as he or she is real to you. But to most human beings the spirit world is unreal because you cannot touch it, you cannot hear it and in many ways you cannot envisage it. When you return to the world of spirit it will seem to you that your experiences on Earth were the unreal ones, because reality is always a matter of confronting what is there before you in the eternal Now.

So let us go back to the beginning of things, to the way in which life came to planet Earth.

Certain spirits — sometimes called 'archons' — move through the cosmos in mysterious ways. Each time a new part of it is to be created, matter is formed by the archons who are responsible for building atomic structure. These beings have the ability to manipulate matter of a specialised kind, such as that found in what you call asteroids. They create — and I am now groping for words — a cosmic dust storm of energy, tiny particles of matter and various other forms of existence. These particles whirl around the asteroids, which form into streams and start to rotate. The microscopic particles in this cosmic dust storm begin to adhere to these asteroids rather like iron filings around a magnet. The process takes millions of years, but eventually this partly physical and partly etheric stream of matter, gases and particles begins to solidify. As it rotates it spirals inward, contracting, causing atomic reactions as the material condenses.

This is a very broad outline, as you will appreciate, but in due course a kind of nuclear fusion takes place and a Sun begins to come into being. As this body spins, all the time becoming more and more dense, particles of it break away and rotate around it.

The rest is much as your scientists envisage — with one notable omission: each solar system must have, as an integral part of its structure, a new belt of asteroids which will absorb the evolutionary code of the system in which they are formed. When that system has completed its evolution they pass on to form another with the knowledge, the experience and the understanding of the previous one recorded in them. Asteroids are, in a sense, the tape recordings or memory bank of a solar system and they are also the seed from which another one grows. They are *not* the remains of a planet that has exploded and been forgotten.

In due course the various bodies that have been cast off by the Sun cool down and become the planets which encircle it. The Sun also attracts other bodies into its field, and thus a solar system with all its attendant bodies is formed. Positive and negative forces are needed to bring such a system into existence: it is created by positive energies and seeded by negative ones — as opposed to your sexual method of pro-creation. If you examine the successive planes of evolution, you will find that these polarising forces are reversed as they descend to each new level: negative-positive, positive-negative and so on. Some very observant person once saw this and depicted it as twin serpents twined round a rod!

All physical life is preceded by — indeed, based on — life in the spirit world: it *must* first manifest higher in the Great Octave before it can do so in matter. Those spirits who guide the development of your solar system have been given many names throughout history — they are the 'Old Ones' who watch over the destiny of entire galaxies. When the archons have fulfilled their task of creating a new solar system, these

'Old Ones' come to guide it and bring it up like a child.

This is no haphazard affair. The great beings who undertake these missions come from other stars in groups; and so it was that a group of beings came to this solar system when it was new. Among them was the Christ spirit, the Solar Logos, the spirit representing the Godhead that looks after this solar system, and other Devas from the sixth plane.

When the Devas first arrive they create an etheric field around a newborn planet. That vibration is then channelled downwards until it has permeated the substance from which physical life will spring. When a planet is to support many forms of life, such as mineral, vegetable, marine, animal and human, all is planned beforehand — an etheric blueprint is first created.

The beings responsible for guiding the evolution of the planet now attract to themselves various groups of spirits from elsewhere in the Universe that wish to experience one of these forms of physical life. So the presiding Deva has no easy task: it has to fashion matter on the planet rather in the way — forgive the analogy — that you cook your cakes: the heat must be just right or they will burn; the mixture must be just right or they will not rise.

Similarly, the prototypes which the Deva creates must allow the various types of visiting spirit to express themselves. Incoming spirits arrive from throughout the Universe, some young in experience and wisdom, others older, and it is the duty of the Deva and, subsequently, the 'Old Ones', to see that the bodies fashioned are suitable vehicles for the expression of the spirits that have come to people the new planet.

During the early stages of a planet's evolution, life is, as you would expect, very primitive. Throughout this period matter is developed and supervised by *the spirits of the elements* that provide the invisible, spiritual thought energy that forms cells into certain shapes, which in turn become primitive organisms. Such early life-forms serve to give expression to the equally primal spirits that help them on to the next stage of their development. When this has been accomplished, these bodies are ready for the next group of spirits to take them over; these are *elementary* spirits, young souls that influence the bodies they enter and, in turn, learn from them. (These elementary spirits should not be confused with *elemental* spirits, spirits of the elements.)

All this time life-forms are being infused by the rays of the Godhead and the Devas that work for it; and so they begin to progress, to assume a form that will lead the physical material of their bodies into the appropriate stream in the planet's eventual design.

It is with the next grade of spirits that the split occurs, as it were, and various branches of the tree diverge. The elementary spirits were rough and ready; knowing no form they simply held the matter together so that a shape could evolve from it, and those spirits who would ultimately find expression on the planet could then take over from them and mould the matter into its intended form.

Watch a potter throw a pot or a vase: he will put his own individual stamp on it, his own artistic trademark as it were. Thus it is with the potter's wheel of life — the hallmark of the spirit is imprinted on the clay which houses it.

Let us say that you have two very primitive bodies which

are neither man nor beast, for such creatures did exist on Earth at one time; into one you introduce a spirit wishing to experience through an animal stream of evolution, and into the other you introduce a spirit gifted with free will which wishes to experience as *homo sapiens*. Each will live a series of lives in its appointed bodies and by the end of that series the two types of body will look very different. One will have grown more fur, developed its instinct and hearing and sense of smell, while the other will have begun to stand erect, to fashion tools, to think and invent and explore. Then each strain will develop along its own line, attracting to itself spirits of its own kind until its species approaches perfection within its bounds. When the species has completed its growth in the evolutionary sense, it will stay put.

And so each branch of evolution bears the hallmark of its potter — the type of spirit that overshadows it. This is why your apes are still apes and have not become men: their spirits are different. Lions and tigers have not become men; the form of life these creatures have chosen has a limited brain capacity and restricted physical experience but *not* a limited instinctual or spiritual experience. The bodies of man and woman have a greater brain capacity, greater powers of intellect and reasoning, but no greater spiritual capacity; in fact, the spirit is all too often inhibited by the intellect. Any incarnating entity is only wise insofar as it uses the body it inhabits to its full capacity, whether that body be furred, feathered, scaled or human. And so evolution proceeds.

There are certain basic chemicals on a planet which can be affected by cosmic radiation. I am not referring to rays coming from the Sun, but to something on a far greater scale.

These radiations are guided and directed by the Deva and its helpers, whose job it is to look after the evolution of a planet. Such radiations may come from another star, another galaxy or, in fact, any part of the Universe. When such a radiation belt passes through a solar system, mutations are caused which can be used by the planetary Deva to implement evolutionary progress.

Let us now return to those early days on Earth. Picture your world composed of rock, dust and water, but with no vegetation at all, no life as you would know it. A gradual transformation took place, humus and vegetation appeared; more chemical changes took place and then came those early forms of life which your scientists have visualised: small creatures like embryos or marine fossils, whose impressions are still to be found in certain rock strata. They gradually evolved until they became animated organisms. Each time a new species comes to a young planet, cosmic radiations are drawn on to assist the process.

Going forward millions of years again, these organisms progressed until they became the mammals, fish and birds you associate with prehistoric times, creatures you consider to be monsters by present-day standards.

As the evolution of the Earth continued, many parts of it cooled and changed until it finally tilted, causing the first ice age. Several axis tilts occurred before the coming of man, but only two have taken place since he emerged. The great creatures who dwelt here during those early times lived vastly different lives from that of the wild animals you know today. If an animal survived the elements it rarely survived its fellows and most species perished during an axis tilt.

And so we move past the epoch of prehistoric monsters and into the age of man. There is much truth in the theories of Darwin, yet his scholarship is seriously flawed by his preoccupation with the evolution of the physical body and his neglect of the spirit or ego. Spiritual evolution and genetic evolution are two entirely different things, which scientists who base all their thinking on material evidence alone, fail to appreciate.

The first land mass that man inhabited was called 'Mu', or the 'Motherland'. During the last century it was given the name 'Lemuria' by a British scientist, after the lemurs. Mu occupied a large portion of the globe, stretching from the Middle East to China and embracing other lands which then extended far into what is now called the Pacific Ocean. However, many of today's continents were then under water, so there was not a preponderance of land. The world bore no resemblance to the picture you now see on your maps, principally because there were no individual land masses.

The continent of Mu flourished for many thousands of years and during this period certain of its inhabitants advanced considerably further than others. These people built cities, the remains of which can still be seen in parts of South America today. These cities were thrown up several thousand feet at the time of the first cataclysm. China, Tibet and pre-dynastic Egypt were Mu-an. Polynesian culture is yet another bearing the hallmark of the first civilisation, and the monolithic edifices on Easter Island, itself once part of Mu, stand like sentinels guarding the secrets of an age long forgotten.

The gulf between the more advanced Muans and those

less evolved grew as time passed. Many of the latter led bestial lives and when the fall came it was the more degenerate parts of Mu that were dashed beneath the waves and boiling lava. Certain external cosmic events caused the Earth's axis to tilt, which brought about the first reversal of the poles and equator to occur during mankind's tenancy of the planet. This did not mean that the entire globe was covered with ice but that the polar regions moved their positions. The evolution of the world was due to take a step forward as it had been at a standstill for some time, and the destruction of the Muan civilisation made way for another, the equal of which has never been known since.

Shortly before Mu was destroyed by this cataclysm, a number of highly evolved spirits incarnated into Muan bodies. As they grew to adulthood the wisdom of their spirits began to manifest and they found that they were far more advanced than those around them. They saw that things were not as they should be and set out to segregate themselves from the bestiality that was rife at the time. They left the continent of Mu and travelled to a distant peninsula which had, until then, been very sparsely populated.

Soon after these pioneers had settled on their new-found land, the catastrophe occurred, causing the face of the globe to change. Another cosmic body passed near to Earth and upset its balance. The results were horrifying. A whole portion of Mu sank beneath what is now the Pacific Ocean; the remaining land masses split and separated into smaller continents. The land upon which the pioneers had settled was spared, though not entirely unaffected: owing to the new position of the Earth in relation to the Sun, climatic conditions throughout the world changed, and they found that they had acquired a fine, warm land. Their peninsula had broken away from the mainland and become an island continent.

Atlantis — for such was the name given to this new continent — grew from strength to strength and, as the millennia went by, achieved a remarkably high state of civilisation.

But the Atlanteans had one cardinal fault. They overdeveloped the philosophical or mystic side of their nature — at the expense of the practical. This left them open to attack and was eventually their undoing. All life experienced in a physical body must be balanced: it must reconcile the spiritual and philosophical with the practical and material. If the balance should tip too far in either direction, downfall will result.

Towards the end of the Atlantean epoch many of the high priests saw what was to come, although the wisest of them realised that it would be for the best in the long run. Unevolved strains from the mainland had infiltrated the younger island people, diverting them from the path of light and, because they had no defence against such things, the islanders' minds were subverted by what you would call black magic — the misuse of energies.

Mass emigrations took place from the ill-fated continent to such places as Egypt, the Middle East, Europe and parts of South and Central America. These emigrants carried with them some of the Atlantean lore, although much of that was to be lost when the next catastrophe occurred.

The Atlanteans' greatest success at colonisation was probably

Egypt for it was to this land, then known as Khemu, that many of the uncorrupted priests took their spiritual and occult knowledge, sowing the seeds of what was later to become dynastic Egypt. It was the Atlanteans who built the original pyramids, using one of the sciences which has long been lost to man: the science of sonics.

However, in returning to the mainland, the Atlanteans were actually returning to the descendants of the Muans from whom they had fled centuries before. Several of the shores on which they landed were far from friendly and countless lives were lost. Those who survived mingled and intermarried with less evolved peoples until most of the Atlantean strains and influences were lost.

The second axis tilt to occur during man's tenure of the Earth brought about the final sinking of Atlantis and was caused by the capturing of the planet Luna, or Lucifer, into the Earth's field, making it a moon. There had been no moon in the sky during the time of Atlantis, as Lucifer had previously enjoyed its own independent course through the solar system.

The Earth is much older than your geologists, anthropologists and archaeologists would have you believe. They have only scratched the surface of the planet's history and, in addition to Mu and Atlantis, there have been many other, lesser civilisations undreamed of by your historians. Mankind has been on this world much longer than is realised. Civilisations have come and gone and their remains lie hidden throughout the globe. As time passes, the remains of these cultures will be unearthed. South America, Australia, even India's ancient history is largely unknown; also Mongolia, parts of China — there were civilisations there long before even the earliest recorded Chinese history — and still others which sank beneath the seas. Some will re-emerge, others have gone for ever, their evolution complete. Even Africa — and not only northern Africa — holds many secrets. In time, some of these will be revealed. And also those of Antarctica.

But that is looking many years ahead.

And so to the present. Mankind is now at a highly materialistic stage and when the pendulum swings, as it surely will in the not-too-distant future, you must be careful not to veer too far in the other direction.

In an ideal society, unevolved spirits would take charge of material things and physical work, more experienced souls would do the work requiring a more subtle understanding, and evolved beings would be in a position of leadership as they are able to translate spiritual knowledge into terms which could be understood by those in their care. It is the pyramid again. Unfortunately, this structure has collapsed and unevolved souls have gained positions of power, as is evidenced by many of your world leaders.

Sadly, thousands of young spirits have had their minds catapulted into the astral world by drugs and the like, and they have not the spiritual training to cope with what they encounter. The effect of this artificial sharpening of the senses is that it tends to illuminate experiences undergone by the spirit in previous lives, and momentarily to reveal dimensions that the mind is unable to grasp, adding to its frustration.

There is a time for enlightenment and a time for pressing onward; short cuts to spiritual experience will rebound in the long run as inner goals have to be worked for.

You may have wondered whether the human being will be the last form of life on Earth. Remember, we started with nothing but the elements and gases, progressed through minerals, rocks, vegetation, marine and animal life and, finally, came to the most devastating of all creatures — man. Is man, who enjoys greater free will than any other species, the ultimate form of life?

As you realise, the world will gradually cool down and undergo cosmic changes until its purpose as a floating university has been fulfilled. Then eventually it will disintegrate and be reabsorbed into the Universe. This will not happen for many, many thousands of years, but it will happen. Then somewhere another solar system or another galaxy will be born and another cycle will start all over again; and yet one cannot say "all over again" because each successive cycle in an ascending spiral is on a slightly higher level.

There is another form of life to come after *homo sapiens*, as there will be etheric life when man no longer lives here. As the Earth grows older, living conditions for mankind on its surface will become more and more difficult. In relation to the dramatic changes of temperature, of land mass and of sea area which take place during the course of the life of a planet, the range of man's endurance is very limited. When the human race finally finds it impossible to withstand the changes occurring, physical existence on Earth will die out until there are merely forms of vegetation once again.

In the final phase of the planet's existence there will still be a very long period from the time when animal and human life disappear to the time when the Earth finally disintegrates. During this period it will be used for spirit evolution, as there are spirits that can gain useful experience on physical worlds. They do not take on bodies for this purpose but simply live on the subtle planes around a planet, learning to understand the meeting point between physcial and etheric life.

32. Ley Lines and Power Centres

Long before the present civilisation, man lived a life that was quite unlike that of today. He was much closer to Nature, in the sense that today he is like a flower that has closed up for the night whereas, in the summer days of the planet's history, man, like the flower, was open. And because he was open, both the natural and cosmic forces that guide this planet were real to him, not as some vague and mystical idea but as something as natural to him as seeing is to you. Early man was aware of no stark division between different life forms nor of a total separation between incarnate and discarnate life, as you see it today.

When these men built their settlements it was only natural that they should wish to communicate with others and so, not having the technology you have now, they formed etheric threads between their towns and hamlets. These threads were either made by the power of their own minds, or by employing natural lines of force encircling the planet. Centres of great importance, of what you would call religious significance, were often built on this natural grid.

As the human population increased, a great network of lines criss-crossed the countryside. Ideas could be relayed along them and, because they were etheric but had been generated from a physical level, it was not long before the ground over which they travelled also began to manifest lines — a perfect example of the etheric manifesting on a material level.

Whenever you have a concentration of mental energy, it duplicates itself at the physical level. And because these lines were positive, constructive and beneficial, the land through which they passed became more fertile, plants grew profusely, animal and insect life was attracted and people built towns and villages along them so that they too could benefit from this force. In due course these lines developed a personality of their own and became living things.

Then, as the autumn of this particular round of evolution approached and the flower of man's mind began to close, he gradually forgot the meaning of these lines. And now, today, you are drawing towards the end of the long dark winter of forgetfulness when life has almost gone, and only a few bulbs remain in the earth here and there. But in these bulbs is a stirring and another spring is not far away. It is time for these plants to re-emerge and blossom once more.

That is my somewhat poetic summary of early life. Perhaps it was not as idyllic as I might seem to indicate, but I have been trying to convey to you that early man's feeling for life and for his surroundings was totally different from your own.

Some of the stronger power lines have remained and these, together with the natural veins of the planet, are what you now call ley lines. If you pursue leys you will find them and, the more sensitive you are, the more you will find. Although most of them have faded away with the passing of time, there is always a faint impression which the more receptive of you will detect. In most countries, the majority of these leys will only lead you to a settlement, then to another and so on. There are others, however, where men tapped the planet's life force for religious purposes.

When the civilisation of Atlantis was coming to an end, many people left the continent as pioneers and journeyed into a comparatively backward world. And yet, remember, what to them was backward was really quite advanced by modern standards — not in terms of technology, but certainly where the understanding of subtle energies is concerned.

They came to Britain in considerable numbers and were able to help the people they found there by showing them how their powers could more efficiently be channelled. But in the long run it was to no avail as man was heading towards the long dark winter I have spoken of.

Man gradually lost touch with this inner knowledge of cosmic energies, but he still remembered that many of these sites were of great importance; the race memory, the group memory lay deep within his subconscious mind; he knew these sites held a great secret, although he no longer knew how or why. But he continued to respect them and wor-shipped his own gods there — perhaps not in the way the original builders would have done, but at least he afforded such places a certain respect.

Those leys which intersect or are near to sites of religious significance are the keys you seek. There was a time when priests believed in and understood what they taught, and tried to expand the consciousness of their flocks — not frighten them into submission. In more recent times, many great churches were built at these sites, because the Church acknowledged their power and wished to claim it for itself. Yet churchmen nowadays cannot handle the power, so they benefit very little from it, simply because they do not understand it.

Some of the places where major lines intersect could be called pumping stations, just as your heart pumps the life fluid through your own veins and arteries. The ancients constructed a grid system whose intersections might be compared with a sub-station on a modern electrical grid. They built stone circles so that the power would enter these circles and rotate before moving on; and in rotating it generated the influence from the particular centre or chakra that that power had immediately come from. (Here I am referring to the chakric system of a country or even of the planet itself: a system of vortices that transform energy between the subtle and the physical, just as you have within your own body.)

The Atlanteans tried to build centres in Britain in order to gather and use the influences from all the planetary chakras, but the system was never completed.

The ancient Britons used these ley lines to a very limited extent: they knew they improved their crops and the health of the people who lived near them, but they did not harness them in the way the Atlanteans themselves did. The Atlanteans intended to harness the power and so realign the chakras that had been thrown out of balance by recent events. They tried to impress on the minds of simple people what they were doing, but it was never really understood, although the Atlanteans were respected in Britain. Often, when people respect others but do not understand them, they imitate the outward displays — which is why these early Britons buried many of their dead close to the Atlantean sites to be near the Old Ones.

Different types of centre give off different kinds of energy. Knowing this, the ancients placed their temples, hospitals and places of learning strategically, to obtain the utmost co-operation from the planet itself. One day you will learn that the ceremonies conducted at these ancient sites were far from the pagan rites your historians and archaeologists would have you believe. All these things will come to light in the coming age, when man will once again learn the art of building his cities and planning his farms, recreation areas and places of celebration in harmony with Nature and the lovely planet upon which he lives.

33. More About Power Centres

As the planet has evolved a number of civilisations have emerged, each with its own type of culture and power. From an inner point of view these powers accumulate with each successive generation. Let us take an imaginary example at a personal level.

If you were to build yourself a little hut at the end of your garden, or to set aside a small room in your house for inner work, you would find that in time an atmosphere would build up, for the power generated in that room or hut would accumulate and make its presence felt. When you do spiritual work such as healing or prayer you create a vortex of energy with its own forcefield which exists over several 'octaves'.

I have indicated that every thought goes out into the Universe to exist there for eternity, gradually decreasing in intensity. Similarly, when you speak, the sound travels away in an ever-widening arc, growing fainter to human ears but nevertheless continuing to exist. It is like a series of circular ripples moving outwards from the spot where a pebble has been thrown into a pond, gradually diminishing as they go.

This is what happens when the average person sends out a thought.

Now, you will have noticed in the above example that I have emphasised the smallness of the hut or room. There is a reason for this: in a confined space you will find it easier to build an atmosphere because the magnetic field of each person easily reaches the corners of the room and rebounds, enabling those taking part to concentrate their thought with greater ease. So, if you repeatedly exercise your thought power in this small hut or room, a forcefield is gradually built up until it begins to have a life of its own.

Suppose that at this point you meet a friend and invite him to your sanctuary, perhaps to do some healing there, then you introduce a third person and the three of you begin to carry out healing work together. All this time the power inside the hut is increasing. You then decide to go away on a holiday, so you lock up, pack your bags and off you go.

While you are away you discover that you have left something important behind in the hut, so you arrange for a friend to drop in and pick it up for you. Now this friend is also psychic and on entering the hut is immediately conscious of a powerful atmosphere, for the simple reason that in your hut you have started a power centre. Those who do psychic work regularly will know that, for this reason, it is a good thing always to use the same room.

This, then, is the way that certain power centres have evolved: by means of the energy accumulated over many years, and in some cases centuries, in one place. Stonehenge is a perfect example of such a centre, although it was later misused and has now fallen into disuse.

Let us now look at another type of power centre, one which originated in a different manner.

Thousands of years ago, your predecessors learned how to manipulate highly potent terrestrial and cosmic forces; possibly the greatest and most powerful of these dynasties flourished in Atlantis. Before Atlantis sank, many were fore-warned of the coming disaster. They also knew that the power they had accumulated over the centuries would retain its potency if it were correctly sealed in suitable locations and a protection were placed around those sites lest anyone stumble on them by accident. For if, in days to come, anyone should accidentally turn the key to such a centre, the accumulated power, unleashed, could be extremely dangerous to the unin-itiated.

So beware, power centre seeker of today, make sure you know what you are doing — because you may release power beyond your imagination, power that you are hopelessly ill-equipped to control.

The story of Pandora's box is, like so many others, no idle myth but a practical warning.

As the final days approached, the reigning Arcanophus sum-moned all the powers used by the priesthood on the Atlantean vibration. He sent priests to seed that power in various parts of the world; and then, by means of certain rituals, he sealed the rays so that none could call upon them until the time came when there would once more be people incarnate on Earth who would possess the right knowledge and wisdom to unseal them. The key to this seal he placed in the land you call England. Its symbol is the sword of St. Michael, or the

Excalibur of Arthur, and its withdrawal signifies the emergence of the new Atlantean race.*

There is a very special reason for this. I must choose my words carefully when I say that the key to this power was sealed in England because that country will have the opportunity — and I stress the word 'opportunity' — to play an important part in future world affairs; not in the field of politics or warfare but as a pathfinder in the struggle to achieve sanity and balance. England has far from reached such a goal and there is a grave danger that it might even veer in the opposite direction, but it is hoped that, as time goes by, the right groups will gradually begin to tap these power centres and use the energies they release to benefit humanity and the world at large.

Where are the power centres? Well, in view of what I have just said, you can hardly expect me to tell you! It is something you must find out for yourselves, either individually or in groups. As you progress, you begin to see and, as you reach finer levels, you begin to understand. That understanding might lead you to one power centre which will in due course lead you to the next. But before you embark on this path, I implore you to be confident that you are equal to the task, that your motives are utterly selfless and that you are capable of handling whatever it is you find behind each successive sealed door. This is of the utmost importance. Both fear and wrong motives will lead you astray.

The key to each power centre is unique and can only be

---

*Here H-A is referring to all those people, of whatever nationality, who are working for mankind and the planet. He is not referring to any group or sect.

turned by inner means. It is something that needs to be approached with humility, patience and care.

If you were to study a map of England, for example, and plot on it details of some of the power centres that are already known, you would find a design emerging. I am not disclosing anything when I refer to such famous sites as Stonehenge, Avebury and Glastonbury; there are many others, perhaps the most important of which are unknown to you. But even by taking the ones that are well known you can begin to build a picture, and from this picture some interesting deductions can be made. You will find a distinct pattern emerging, one that reflects the evolution of the Earth itself. And likewise, in other countries there are similar patterns waiting to be discovered.

The power waiting to be tapped at these sources could generate peace and confidence among the peoples of the world, adding impetus to the forces of Light in this ever-intensifying battle between harmony and chaos.

34. The Spirits of the Elements

When a new thought or spirit first leaves the Godhead, it has the gift of free will to experience in whichever way it wishes. Some spirits choose human existence, others decide to enter the animal, vegetable or mineral kingdom. There are other streams of evolution that do not require a physical body at all, yet which affect your everyday life even though you may be totally unaware of them.

Very few people today give much thought to what may appear to be mere processes of Nature; the vast majority of men and women neither see nor hear the beings or intelligences that express themselves by serving the planet at this level.

The spirits of fire, air, earth and water are collectively known as 'the spirits of the elements' and individually as 'elementals'. The names given to these beings by the ancients were: 'salamanders' for spirits of fire, 'sylphs' for spirits of the air, 'ondines' or 'nymphs' for water spirits and 'gnomes' for earth spirits. Some people, either by training themselves in the art of perception or by means of a natural gift, are able to see these creatures and observe the part they play. The beauty and innocence of children often attract them, so please do not scold or laugh at the child who claims to have seen some 'little people', for it may well be true.

Earth elementals are often seen as gnomes of varying sizes and appearances, while air elementals sometimes appear as fairies with wings. It must be understood, however, that *it is man who has created these images of his elemental cousins, not the elementals themselves*; they merely adopt a guise by which they will be recognisable to human beings. A child would not connect a gnome with a lump of quartz or a sylph with a beam of light. The forms that they adopt for recognition will probably change as man's concept of them changes.

Elemental spirits do not evolve in the same manner as mankind. They begin their evolutionary journey as a single element or as part of the group soul of a particular element and, as they advance, they become more and more individualised. Normally the group soul of an element stays intact and does not individualise unless for some special purpose or job. When an elemental has learnt all that it can of its own element it begins to seek experience in one of the other three. These it will master one at a time; so, although many elementals are of a single nature, others have a twofold or threefold nature. Once an elemental masters all four elements it is said to have won its fourfold nature, whereupon it ascends to the planes of the Devas and will assist in the guidance of planets.

Human spirits are also fourfold by nature, but these four aspects are not as individually accentuated as they are in a fourfold elemental or Deva.

An elemental can quicken its evolution by serving a living person. For example, a salamander can learn patience or a sylph the meaning of emotion from being close to a human being: both being qualities they would normally lack. This has given rise to many legends about fairies gaining immortality — their fourfold nature — by 'marrying' (joining with) mortals.

As you move through your lives and meet different types of people with their various character traits and affinities, you will notice that some, for example, are attracted to water, while others dislike it. There are those who love the bite of a keen wind or the heat of the Sun on a summer's day. There are those who love mountains, while others feel instinctively hemmed in and oppressed by them. Many people dislike extremes of heat or cold, and others carry their aversion to air elementals so far that the slightest draught is a source of annoyance to them. Study your friends' likes and dislikes; you will soon be able to discern which of the elements they are in harmony with and which make them feel ill at ease and this will deepen your understanding of them.

Although each person will always have an affinity with one or more elements in particular, not only as a preference but as an integral part of his or her physical and psychological make-up, a sympathy with all four elements should be developed.

Many fears of the elements are of a karmic nature and stem from being drowned or crushed in a previous life, or perhaps from being burnt. Some of these traumas are man's own fault, resulting from his misuse of the facilities offered him by nature, while others are related to such events as landslides, volcanic eruptions and floods and are, therefore, less directly his responsibility. When man has learned to understand and co-operate with his elemental cousins, many natural hazards will be prevented. The animal kingdoms, which are in closer touch with these spirits, exemplify this: notice how they will sense a coming earthquake and evacuate an area long before it occurs. Even man's most sophisticated equipment can only record a tremor, it cannot anticipate it.

The influence of the elementals on the Earth has been somewhat undermined by the misguidance the planet has been suffering. When the rightful Deva returns to guide planet Earth, the elemental influences will be felt much more strongly and this will greatly benefit mankind as a whole.

Although, like yourselves, these beings are composed of thought, they operate on a 'sharper' frequency than mankind and one that is radioactive by nature. Elementals can communicate with man and achieve the best results by telepathically transmitting thought pictures to the mind of a sensitive person, which he or she can translate into words. It would pay you handsome dividends to develop this affinity with the spirits of the elements and work in co-operation with them, for you could learn much about your planet and how to cope with it in a natural way.

You will appreciate that these beings are not perfect and are learning just as you are. They make mistakes as you do, hence the physical evolution of the world has not always been as smooth as might be desired. But they are still very actively concerned with the planet.

Do these elemental spirits ever incarnate into human bodies and, if so, does their essential nature effect the body they enter?

The answer is yes, they can in special circumstances enter the human lifestream, and do so to undertake a specific task. Of all the elementals, fire spirits or salamanders are most uncomfortable in human bodies — they find the control of physical energy extremely difficult because, like the element they represent, they tend to leap into action with an explosive vigour only to burn low almost to an ember until refuelled. Fire tends to consume all obstacles in its path, which in human existence is impossible; consequently the incarnate fire elemental takes more than his or her fair share of knocks. Fire is the creative element.

Water elementals are more adaptable. They flow round life's obstacles and do not attempt to meet them head-on. However, although possessing a more serene and equable temperament than their fiery cousins, they can stagnate which is equally undesirable.

The incarnate air elemental has boundless energy. Perhaps he or she does not show this in the obvious way — it may manifest in a quieter person as sheer stamina, but it is present nevertheless. These people do not like staying still; they are always full of ideas and often gifted with words with which to express them. They are progressive, even visionary, although lacking the practical stability of the earth elemental.

Earth elementals are stubborn and possessive yet they can be the charmers of the elemental kingdom; they possess that infinite patience that enables them to plumb the very depths of a person's character without being put off by abrupt externals. Although they may appear slow, they usually get there in the end. They are the moulding and stabilising element.

Incarnate elementals of a single nature will betray their origin by their one-track approach to life. Incarnate Devas are more able to present an appearance of the normal fourfold nature of man, although in times of stress they tend to fall back on their original element as a last line of defence — or attack!

35. The Deva Kingdoms

Let us now follow the progress of a spirit that has gained its fourfold nature by mastering all four elements — fire, earth, air and water — and ascends to the kingdom of the Devas.

The word 'deva' comes from the Sanskrit term meaning 'shining one' and was originally bestowed on those beings who, in Christianity, are known as angels. This is a branch of evolution quite apart from that of man that does not normally incarnate into physical bodies — although in special circumstances it is possible for them to do so.

There are many types of Deva and the early Christian fathers gave them names and divided them into nine 'choirs'. To label them thus is limiting and misleading, but the early fathers were simply trying to indicate that certain types of angel are responsible for specific tasks in the evolutionary scheme of things. Cherubim, for example, are responsible for the growth and ascendancy of *homo sapiens*; archons are the controllers of atomic structure, while seraphim are the cleansers or fiery ones.

A planet is usually guided by a group of devas with one presiding. This group will consist of representatives of all the many choirs of angels. Thus the retinue of the governing Deva of a planet such as Earth will include devas who will help man, those who will watch over the animal kingdom, devas of plant and insect life and those that govern the seasons and elements. All these lifestreams are interdependent, complementary.

This is something you will have to re-learn, since you have regrettably lost sight of the part played by other intelligences in the everyday running of your planet!

This may lead you to ask, "Is the Deva using a planet to advance its own evolution, and does it progress with that world?" My answer would be that both are true — if the Deva is wise enough. But this is not so in every case.

You have a great barrier to overcome on Earth at the present time, because the devic influence is not as it should be: an alien, malign influence is attempting to sidetrack the overall evolution of the planet from its rightful path. This makes it difficult for many people to cope with their own lives. Your immediate reaction to this might be, "How can *I* help? Surely that is out of my hands?" But is it? Remember, everything you do, say and think is either helping or hindering the rightful Deva. By your thoughts and actions you can feed either the forces of Light or those of darkness. *It is in your own hands!*

From this you will see how all things influence each other. Whenever you perform an action you are affecting the overall destiny of the planet because you are a complementary part of it; because of that, you are also affecting the entire solar system. This system is an integral part of the Universe so, like it or not, what you do in your life affects the whole Universe!

36. Planetary Guidance

What is it that gives a planet its unique character?

All physical manifestation has a form of spirit life which guides, animates and controls it.

In the case of a planet, it is the spirits of the elements that mould its form and express themselves through the physical matter and gases of which it is composed, under the supervision of the planetary Deva, a spirit of advanced evolution. It is the overall emanations from the Devas, blending with the physical vibrations of the planets in their charge, that have been observed and have given birth to the much-maligned and misunderstood science you know as astrology. Here you have the inner reality behind the subject.

What is Earth's role in the solar family?

Earth is the planet of Music and Healing; these are both its inner qualities and its outer influence. Every tribe and every civilisation throughout the world and throughout time have included in their culture to a marked degree both music and healing.

Music, like any other energy, can be used for any and every purpose. It can soothe, heal, inspire and uplift — or it can unsettle, overstimulate and degrade. The Ancients understood both the creative and destructive powers of music and, in some civilisations, certain types of music were forbidden because they were considered to have a degenerating effect. Those wise ones knew that music, through the effect of its harmonies and rhythms on the mind and emotions of man, even has the power to *sustain* or *destroy* a civilization! So choose your music wisely and allow it to heal you, balance you and inspire you.

As all the planets and their Devas are in varying stages of evolution, so are the influences they exert benign or otherwise, according to their relationships with each other and with the Earth at any given moment.

I would emphasize that each of the planets is guided, not controlled, by its respective Deva, and that although every species has the free will to accept or reject the Deva's guidance, its influence is of a powerful nature and will affect the overall character of the planet.

OUR UNIVERSE

37. The Ever-evolving Universe

You said there was no beginning and no end to the Universe. Can you enlarge on this?

The Universe is ever-changing; it always was and always will be. The supreme Intelligence behind it maintains a perpetual flow to and from itself. The stars, systems and galaxies of the visible Universe will have an ending insofar as the physical matter of which they are composed will cease to exist in that state. But they will not truly end: the atoms of which they consist will increase in speed or vibration and form a new chain of existence in a dimension beyond the grasp or comprehension of the human mind.

The graduation of atoms from one dimension to another sets up a friction which in turn brings into being an entirely new set of atoms. These newly-created atomic structures are of a similar, but not identical, pattern and 'weight' to those of the Universe which has dissolved. Thus another galaxy is born, another set of suns and stars comes into being for future generations of intelligences to survey with whatever instruments they might possess. The density or vibration of this new galaxy differs from the old one by only the slightest fraction. Thus the experiences to be gained within it vary from those of its predecessor, as no evolutionary plan is identical or repetitive.

The Universe did not start with a colossal bang. Nor is it constantly spreading outwards leaving a hole in its centre, as some theorists will have you believe. If this can be expressed in words, there is one central atom which is perpetually expanding from its core. As it does so, it fuses with other elements in the cosmos and from this continual fusion Universes — collections of galaxies — are born. In time, these Universes raise their atomic vibration and are absorbed into the original core, creating as they do so yet other Universes. Thus is the unending flow of creation maintained. Nothing is ever lost. The cosmos is forever expanding in a dimension beyond those of time and space. Eventually, as mankind evolves, it will take in more of this picture.

38. A Glimpse of the Plan

The Plan for the Universe is: Evolution, with the Godhead as the ultimate goal. In order to expand in its infinity, the Godhead gives birth to creative thought that undergoes an entire cycle of evolution, unique unto itself, and finally returns in complete wisdom and harmony to its Source.

Let us look a little deeper into this law of Evolution. When a thought leaves the Ultimate it descends to a plane even lower than that of Earth. Picture, if you will, an inverted hollow cone. The top of this cone extends upward to such a height that its rim borders on the infinite. The new thought, having left the Ultimate, descends to the bottom of this cone. At this point it has no evolutionary record and only a limited comprehension. It is as a seed, with infinite potential. As realisation dawns, it begins to rise up the cone and, the higher it reaches, the wider grow its horizons of perception and the less it is restricted by its surroundings. It can start to ascend at any angle, or travel horizontally, or even descend again if it so desires: its free will to choose is another cosmic law in itself.

That innermost striving of a spirit to uplift itself, to

advance and grow, is often reflected on Earth as a desire to improve such things as one's surroundings and one's standards.

As a spirit ascends the cone in an ever-widening spiral, it gains in an infinite number of ways. But should it at any time lose its directional impulse, the higher it has reached, the further will it fall. It is not unknown for spirits from the fifth or even sixth plane to fall right to the bottom.

If a spirit retrogresses and then by spiritual endeavour regains its former state, it experiences, in fact, more fully than its fellows whose evolution has followed a comparatively smooth spiral. But in the process it will have caused itself great suffering and lived through many hells of its own making.

Picture a large crowd moving in one direction. One man is trying to push his way through this crowd in the opposite direction. His movements — which can range from a gentle push to a violent shove — affect not only his own path but also those people he is obliged to push aside and even hurt in order to achieve his objective. You can see from this analogy the effect created by a spirit choosing to go against the directional impulses of cosmic law. The damage to itself and others can be inconceivable.

A highly-evolved being is one that is able to control the directional flow of its creative energies. In other words it has exercised its free will in such a way as to enable it to withstand the negative attractions of lower levels of thought. You will appreciate from this how essential it is from an evolutionary point of view to maintain balance and harmony.

39. The Significance of the Sun

Have you ever wondered if it is merely its physical properties that makes the Sun so warm and comforting? If you go back to earlier civilisations you will find that many peoples in the past have worshipped the Sun. Today this may seem rather strange, eccentric, even primitive behaviour. But it was none of these. I am not going to suggest that you rush out immediately and kneel in the rays of the Sun — far from it! But the people of those times were aware of the Sun's inner significance because, in one respect, they had an even greater knowledge of the Universe than you have today.

The Sun is in every sense the parent or giver of life to your solar system. From its immense gaseous body emanated each planet in turn. I must qualify this by reminding you that there are other masses within the solar system that are not regarded by your astronomers and scientists as planets because they are too small; and, to be precise, many of these bodies did not emanate from the Sun but were attracted or 'captured' by its powerful magnetic field.

Since each of the planets in the solar family has emerged

from the Sun, you will appreciate that everything that happens to each of them affects the Sun and, conversely, everything that takes place in and around the Sun affects these planets. Everything you think, feel and do as an individual has an effect, however small, on your entire world and on the Sun itself!

You can see how the whole solar system is a compact unit, somewhat similar in structure to an atom.

Not only is the Sun a giver of warmth and light, but it carries with it a rare and potent vibration. Spiritually, this could be likened to the fifth spirit plane, the plane of light and colour, for here a spirit may experience its last contact with a physical frequency before ascending to the realms of pure spirit. For centuries, Earth scientists have tried to assess the nature of the Sun and, in the main, they have fallen short because the elements concerned are quite beyond the scope of their instruments.

The Sun is a great deal larger in my estimation than in yours, because around its visible body are planes of existence beyond your own range of frequencies. If you could see them with the naked eye you would notice that these planes encompass the entire solar system and that you and the Earth exist within them: you are, in fact, all part of the Sun. What you see when you look through your sunglasses is, in reality, only the core of the Sun and I would not regard it as being separate from your own world.

The Sun itself has a form of guidance, the Solar Logos — that part of the Godhead which is responsible for this particular solar system. When a spirit passes on from the sixth plane to the seventh or Ultimate plane it enters an infinity of dimensions, as the Godhead itself is without beginning and without end. I would describe it to you — while conceding that there are no words to equal the task — as being an infinite Thought. Every lower plane of existence is part of it, and yet this Thought extends beyond those planes to a state of perfection beyond your comprehension. The Godhead in its infinity is continually evolving.

That which is all-wise is becoming wiser.

The guiding force behind the Sun is a manifestation, an ambassador one might say, of the Godhead and represents a threshold leading to the seventh plane. Thus, when your ancestors worshipped the Sun they were obeying a deep, instinctive understanding — and were not merely revering a cosmic power station that gave them light and heat!

You were once High Priest of the Sun in Atlantis. Would you give us any other observations you have on the Sun and its function in this Solar System?

The Sun is a living Being, an embodiment of the principles of Light, Love and Power, and in order to bring these guiding forces into manifestation it has taken on its present guise.

Beyond your own is another, even greater Sun; and beyond that, another, and so on. Each of these great Beings is a gigantic transformer, filtering or stepping down the cosmic energy it is constantly receiving, so that members of its own system or family can benefit from its awesome power.

If each of these Suns can be described as giving off its own individual note, then together they are sounding a great chord of unimaginable purity and power — and here lies a mystery you will eventually decipher.

40. The Planets in the Solar System

If you include the Moon — which was once a planet in its own right — there are twelve planets in your solar system: those with which you are already familiar plus two others which are not generally acknowledged but of whose existence there is ample scientific evidence. One of these 'new' planets, Vulcan,* has an orbit between the Sun and Mercury; while the other, Persephone,* is at the outer edge of the solar system beyond Pluto.

The solar system as a whole is in a state of balance, just as all creation must be in balance in order to function properly; therefore if any one member of a cosmic family behaves erratically, it has an effect on the others. Individually, each planet completes cycles of evolution in the same way as you yourselves do. At present, as you are doubtless aware, Earth is

---

*Before these two planets were officially named, H-A gave them the titles Orpheus (Vulcan) and Pan (Persephone) to denote their inner quality.

passing through the final stages of a necessarily materialistic phase of its development. But in undergoing this particular experience, man has lost his balance and his drifted towards an extreme: he is becoming *dangerously* materialistic. He is limiting himself — blinding himself — and it is urgently necessary for all those who can see even the merest glimmer of light to try to cure this blindness.

Soon the Earth will reach the moment when it must take another step forward and, as I have already suggested, when this test or initiation has taken place, the human race must ensure that the pendulum does not swing back too far in the opposite direction — that of spirituality that has not been earthed in practical and material realities.

Man has to keep one foot firmly on the ground. You cannot avoid physical experience, nor can you ignore your spiritual obligations, but should try to find the ideal harmony between the two. This you must do not only for your own sake and that of the other species living on Earth, but for the sake of the planet itself and the delicate balance between it and the other members of the solar family.

Each of your planetary neighbours has an inner vibration or quality relating to its specific role in the solar family. And, hence, each planet also has an outer or astrological influence which relates broadly to its inner quality.

Planet	Inner quality	Outer influence
SATURN	philosophy	limitation, consolidation
PERSEPHONE	natural law	growth
URANUS	science, technology	sudden happenings, awakenings
MERCURY	mental receptivity, learning, knowledge	communication, intellect
VULCAN	art, creativity	disciplined creativity
NEPTUNE	mysticism, appreciation of subtle energies	sensitivity, dissolving
EARTH	music and healing	music and healing
MOON	the mind and the emotions	responsiveness and fluctuation
JUPITER	judgment	expansion, preservation
PLUTO	peace, the subconscious mind	elimination, regeneration, transformation
MARS	industry, energy	initiatory force, activation
VENUS	love, harmony and beauty	unification and harmonisation

You still have much to learn about your planetary neighbours, and even about the Moon: although astronauts have landed on its surface, there are many things there that they have not yet discovered and, if I may say so, many other things they *have* found and have not told you about! And although man is sending reconnaissance vehicles of a mechanical kind to the other planets, it will not be too long before this unwieldy method of space travel will finally be rejected in favour of means of propulsion more in keeping with the laws of the Universe.

OUR WAY AHEAD

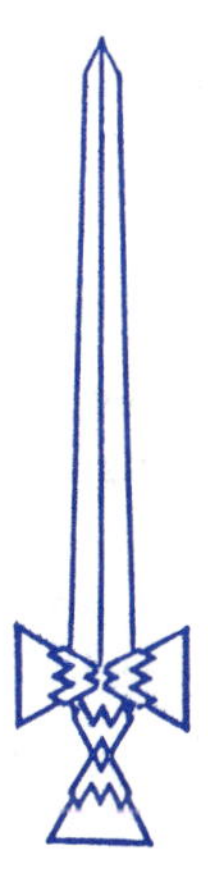

41. Co-creators in the Great Experiment

There is so much ranged against us in life today. Do we really have the means to find our way through it all?

Long ago, a wise man said — and who am I to have a better formula? — ''Man, know thyself''. In these three words lie all the answers to your problems, from the personal to the global. Investigate yourself, and what do you find? That you are a synthesis of all creation, of all the kingdoms, both physical and subtle:

You are *matter* — atoms, molecules, cells, organs all in constant motion

You are *energy* — and who would deny that!

You are *mineral* — your body contains a high proportion of minerals, chemicals and trace elements

You are *water* — almost all water; and was not the sea the laboratory from which life first emerged on Earth?

You are *vegetable* — your intestinal flora, for instance

You are *animal* — armed with primal instincts, means of attack and defence, and a body with which to explore and manipulate your surroundings

You are *human* — the midway point or fulcrum of all life; a synthesis of all the energies, higher and lower; self-aware

You are *emotion* — a highly effective system or overdrive that gives you colour, depth and dimension

You are *mind and intelligence* — which is your very own infinity machine

You are *will* — a fantastic gift which can help you achieve the near-impossible; or, if misused. . .

You are *spirit* — part of which is with you here on Earth, while part remains in the higher worlds. It is your permanent link with the Divine

You are *love* — the light within you that you hide or shield — or allow to illumine everyone and everything around you

Combine all these and you are co-creators with God in the great experiment called Life.

Now, just exactly how you use these resources to surmount the challenges must remain for you yourselves to decide. No-one can and no-one will drop all the answers in your lap, for such would be to cheat you of the purpose of your lives! But here is a clue, and one I beg you not to overlook:

Do not dismiss the simple or the seemingly obvious.

You love to complicate. You love going the long and hard way round. In your thought and philosophy and science you have a taste for elaborate tangles — the more intricate and difficult they are to dismantle, the happier you seem to be!

You strive for position, power, importance, based on ego, and you neglect the honest, inner promptings that can lead you to the fullest expression of yourself, to finding out who you really are and allowing yourself simply to be and to grow. You disregard the power of your hearts and let your intellect and ambition lead you by the nose.

There is another way...

42. The Greatest Power of them all

It has been said that, "Love is the greatest power of them all."
Is this literally true?

Without any question. It is scientific fact, not poetic fantasy. Just as white is a synthesis of all the colours in the spectrum, so love is the perfect synthesis of wisdom, will and intelligence.

It is the ultimate energy, embracing and sustaining all others. It is the fuel that drives the very wheelwork of Nature, the current running through the machinery of the Universes, both physcial and subtle. Remove it, even for an instant, and the entire cosmos would collapse.

As you have discovered, to experience life fully you must give and receive, so that a flow is created. To become complete you have to give love and to receive it; you have to achieve understanding and to pass it on; and so forth, on every level. Do one without the other and an imbalance is created. Take all the time but never give, and you become a miser — not necessarily in the monetary sense, but maybe a spiritual or emotional miser. Go about blindly giving away here, there and everywhere — and you reveal your lack of inner strength, your hunger for love and approval. There are many people of both kinds. It would be difficult to say which of the two is the sadder.

When you have experienced the healing and exhilarating power of love — and by 'love' I mean something more beautiful and selfless than the possessive emotion that so often masquerades as love — when you have felt the extraordinary benefits of giving *and* receiving that finer love, I urge you to release some of this power not only to your own circle of loved ones but also to your fellow beings, known and unknown — making sure you do not leave out the animal, plant and mineral kingdoms who serve you so unselfishly.

If I had only shared a brief moment with you — instead of enjoying your friendship for several years — I could not have given you a more important message than this:

Whatever else you do, learn to love and co-exist with Nature.

Plants, trees, flowers and herbs give you more than you have ever imagined. But these gifts should be neither demanded nor stolen from the great living Being that is Earth; they should be exchanged.

"Exchanged for what?" you ask.

For your kindness, care and co-operation. If the truth be known, the very sight, sound and smell of human beings — with honourable exceptions, of course! — fill the Nature kingdoms with horror and revulsion.

When a man *does* achieve a harmony and friendship

with Nature, you can immediately sense it in him as it gives him a kind of serenity, a settled and kindly approach to life.

Do all in your power, then, in whatever way you are able, to restore the balance between yourselves and the ever-patient, endlessly generous planetary Being who sustains you. Is not her patience and her generosity — despite your persistent cruelty to her — the ultimate proof of her love?

It is the spiritual seed, that spark of God that has been planted within each of you, that is your true self. But because of physical conditioning, the limitations of the body and the environment in which you live, that seed which is truly you becomes lost, submerged. You no longer recognise it. You do not see it, you do not hear its voice, you do not express it . . . But gradually if you allow the unfolding process to take place, that true beauty will begin to manifest itself again.

At this very moment a great awakening is taking place. A rapidly growing number of you are starting to see that beauty within yourselves, within each other and within the Earth itself. It is a shift in consciousness, a shift at the very core of your being.

This transformation is being encouraged by many unseen friends — spirits such as myself who came to plant a seed many years ago that only now is starting to flower. The spiritual impulse lying within every single living cell is being challenged to come forward — *now*. It requires hard work, tolerance, commitment — and real love. Not a surface love, but one expressed by the *whole* of you — to yourself, to each other, to mankind, to the planet. And it must be present in your every thought and action.

With that love radiating from you, *you* will undergo a

transformation. With that love, Earth will at last have the peace and harmony she craves, as will all the other kingdoms that live within, upon and around her.

Love is the key. The only key that will open the door to your survival.

43. The Second Coming

People talk about the Second Coming of Christ. Will it happen and, if so, how?

There have been many prophecies made about a return of the Christ. May I say here and now that what is happening on your planet at this time is not a situation in which any one single figure will emerge as a world visionary or leader, because present-day experience is moving beyond that concept.

The rhythm in which humanity is progressing at this present time is such that people are beginning to approach each other in their understanding of the Universe. A tolerance is slowly emerging between different beliefs. It would be quite wrong to try to force a dominant view of spirituality on mankind today. Indeed, one of the features of the imbalance which has been brought about by the wrongful guidance of the planet is a form of personal worship, because a spirit that is 'bent' can only exist by domination, by having power over others. It needs to create fear, it needs to create idolatry; it wants people to worship a person or a name rather than allowing them to unfold and flower through their own free will seeking.

This unbalanced influence seeks expression through those who would set themselves up as antigods, the 'prophets' who offer you aggrandisement and a quick, easy way to higher consciousness; who offer you the universe on a plate if you will follow them. God will never do this because each of you has been given absolute freedom of spirit to seek and to find in whatever way you will. You as an individual have that free will to accept or reject any mortal thing at any moment in your life.

The Christ spirit, the Christ impulse, as I prefer to call it, is already approaching. It is increasing here amongst you at this very moment, bringing wisdom and Light wherever people are ready to receive it *and whatever their religion*. And as it increases, souls of greater wisdom and evolution are able to incarnate to strengthen it and serve on Earth as the millennium approaches.

Despite the darkness, the Light *is* increasing and is coinciding with the emergence of the new age. Great forces of Light are helping Michael to regain his rightful guardianship as Deva of Planet Earth.

Open your hearts and minds for it is through *you* that the Christ impulse needs to manifest. *You* can bring it about!

44. The Avatars

Almost all the known Avatars or prophets who have guided us throughout history seem to have been men. Is there any chance that one might be a woman?

This sounds rather a male question! Forgive me, do not be offended, I know what prompted you to ask this.

Man is essentially the *outward* expression of humanity, and woman the *inward.* There are many exceptions, of course, and countless variations, but in essence that is the complementary function of the sexes.

Now you might not have heard of them, but many, many great women have lived on Earth and brought wisdom and spiritual nourishment to mankind that was not so obvious or so widely reported as the teachings of the great male Avatars.

It must have occurred to you that all the Masters who have incarnated on Earth have had to come through the body of a woman — a woman of high spiritual degree. The maternal wisdom and example of these women was often the true power behind the historic teachings of their illustrious sons.

Indeed, I would go further: in my view much of the wisdom given to the world by the great Avatars came directly from the women behind them. But a patriarchal, male-oriented society would not be prepared to accept its spiritual leadership from a woman, so the women acting as necessary polarities of these great teachers played an unsung or sacrificial role.

The contribution of men in human history has largely been one of exploration and invention, often with positive effects and sometimes with disastrous ones. Women have been the preservers, the custodians of continuity, exerting a mellowing and compassionate influence where it is so often needed. And so we can see that, where men have provided the will and intelligence necessary for man's survival and development, women have supplied the love and wisdom essential in such an enterprise.

So, with respect, the very concept of male Avatars is a misleading one!

Why not begin to recognise and appreciate both the male and female qualities within yourselves, each one of you, and seek to discover your own inner teacher or Avatar through a proper balance of those energies?

Your own spirit awaits you!

45. Can Mankind Survive?

Can we survive this crisis point in our life on Earth?

In his attempt to subjugate Nature, man is taking on something he by no means fully understands and is disconcerted when nature reacts in what he considers to be a perverse or unco-operative way! I do not intend to elaborate on the many harmful results of pollution as you are already beginning to feel the effects of this in your own life. Lakes and seas have been despoiled and the balance of the oceans is being seriously disturbed; and this is only one of the elements. Man has created toxic gases which kill off all vegetation. He over-works the soil, laying waste to vast areas, destroying forests, creating dustbowls and unnatural desert land. He sprays living organisms with toxic chemicals, many of which will take decades to lose their effect. He manufactures indestructible plastics which, while they seem to make a valuable contri-bution to your life today, are already creating problems for coming generations. Materials that do not blend with the natural process of growth and dissolution are out of balance with the rest of nature — a consideration that has been callously ignored.

For all his creative genius, man seems unable to evisage and to plan for the future. By living for today he is plunging himself and his children head-first into a major catastrophe. He is forcing his body to perform in a way that was never intended. Fortunately, nature is adaptable and resilient and has gallantly accommodated man's abuses, but the increasing acceleration is forcing it to its limits.

Many people are no longer prepared to accept natural forms of experience. Instead of approaching the inner realms by means of learning and guidance, they want instant results fuelled by drugs and artificial stimulants. While the phenomena produced in this way may provide temporary mental entertainment, no true spiritual experience is ever achieved because that can come only with inner development.

By seeking lazier forms of entertainment, and by allowing others to do their thinking for them, people are drifting into a state of zombieism; they are forfeiting their individuality.

But ask yourself: why is all this happening? Because, like the people whom they lead and whom they do not encourage to think, leaders and profiteers are not concerned with the future. They are only concerned with the power they can wield over their fellow men *now*.

Throughout recorded history, isolated patches of evil have erupted on Earth like boils on an unhealthy skin, in the shape of tribal and racial wars, inquisitions, persecutions and massacres. When the Christ light was all but extinguished, Europe sank into the Dark Ages — century after century of infamy, terrorism and torture. And today famine, oppression, espionage, murder, robbery, violence, sexual excess, drug-trafficking and cruelty to women and children have reached such a pitch throughout society that it could almost be said that the lower astral planes have erupted into the physical plane.

A gruesome scenario indeed, but I make no apology for presenting it: you would not thank me for offering you bland reassurances and benedictions at this planetary Moment.

Such are the problems you are up against.

So. Are you apathetic? Or are you making some effort to help by bringing kindness, fairness, tolerance and balance into your everyday life? It is easy to push your way through life, but not so easy to stand back and let someone else walk before you.

Let us try to do something before it is too late.

I urge you to use whatever position or influence you may enjoy to bring *active* kindness, fair play and tolerance to those around you.

Every minute events are taking place that are dragging the Earth closer and closer to an inevitable climax. If something is not done soon, the rape of earth, air and water will have passed the point of no return. I wonder how many scientists understand what will happen if the pollution of the seas and the destruction of the forests really get out of hand. Oxygen is a precious commodity and if man is not careful there could be a serious shortage of it.

The future of this planet is not rigidly preordained: it follows a certain pattern, but you have the choice — and the power — to shape it either way.

You must now *make* that choice.

46. You Want to Change the World? Start with Yourself!

You have often said that changes must be made if we are to survive. How can we set about making such enormous changes in so little time?

Change can only spring from within yourself, from an adjustment in your thinking and a simplifying of your life. Life need not be complicated at all, and it is for this very reason that I speak on what might appear to be a rather elementary level, because it is at this level, surprisingly perhaps, that the foundation of wisdom is to be found.

True wisdom does not lie hidden in a maze of secrecy and mysticism or in clouds of high-flown intellectual concepts, or in ever-more-complex technology. It lies in simplicity and understanding — an understanding that can affect your every thought, word and action in everyday life.

It is all a question of balance or equilibrium. Have you found yours? How can you set about finding it? Are you afraid of life or do you accept it? Do you accept yourself for what you are? Are you afraid of other people? Being *un*afraid does not mean being insulting and objectionable to others — those who go around in this manner are the very ones who *are* afraid, as they are not really sure of themselves. And this applies to nations, of course, as well as individuals. There is nothing wrong with being sure of yourself, provided that surety brings with it tolerance and understanding.

Let us pursue this even further. Are you honest with yourself, and with the people around you? If you do something wrong, are you able to admit it and face up to it? If so, you will learn a valuable lesson from the experience.

I hope you will forgive such a roundabout answer to your simple question — but it is often the simple question that leads into the widest territory!

When the human race as a whole emerges into the light of the coming age, reacquaints itself with such basic aspects of universal law as karma and reincarnation and begins to instil this wisdom into its children, such dangerous follies as ruthless competition, male chauvinism, hoarding of resources and money, intrigue, espionage and war will fade into oblivion, or linger as sobering reminders of a long and troubled and mercifully receding past.

And what will have replaced them? A far more rewarding set of principles and activities, such as:

    — self-acceptance, self-respect, self-responsibility
    — thinking for yourself
    — respect for others, their opinions and beliefs regardless of race, colour, religion or occupation.
    — respect for planet Earth and all its life forms

— education based on the development of the human character and the unfolding of the essential spirit within each child
— business based on mutual advantage
— sharing and cooperating
— a growing awareness of both the material and subtle universes
— loving and forgiving

And not a century too soon!

47. The Turning Point

A lot of people sense that this particular period is more than just the transition from one century to another, but something far greater. Do you agree?

Indeed, yes. The evidence is everywhere around you. Seen from a cosmic perspective, man has been steadily descending into the material, has immersed himself as far as it is possible to go, and is now poised for the long climb back into the Light.

In the years that lie immediately ahead, you are going to have to face the supreme challenge — one that will decide once and for all whether the forces of Light are going to illuminate every corner of the planet or whether opposing forces will drag it down into darkness.

Man has learnt much during this century. He has gained knowledge concerning nuclear power, the atom and the fundamental outer structure of all things. He has learnt much about electronics. He is beginning to rediscover certain ways of using sound and vibration and thought, and how all these things play a part in the universal economy. He has begun to understand time in relation to other dimensions.

The acquisition of knowledge urgently needs to be tempered with wisdom and responsibility and so, during the coming years, it will require even greater efforts on the part of all of you to spread the good word, bearing in mind that in doing so you will have the help of powerful unseen friends.

During this period there is a strong possibility of major geophysical changes and upheavals. This is *not* a foregone conclusion but highly probable. If it happens it will be the direct result of man's behaviour over the centuries. This is clearly a situation Nature cannot allow to continue. A moment will be reached when suddenly the pendulum will swing the other way.

Everything is now hanging in the balance within man's mind and heart, within his very soul: the balance between good and evil, the balance between love and fear. If fear wins, then war and holocaust will follow. If love wins, there will still be problems but they will be greatly minimised.

Whatever happens, there will be great change. There will be climatic disturbances causing agricultural and communications problems in several countries. There will be abrupt changes of leadership throughout the world — and this is already starting to take place.

Change is manifesting in many ways and on many levels, as the human conscience awakens and people begin to demand the truth. This is causing instability in the governments of the world and many leaders are finding themselves in very precarious positions.

Deep down within the soul of mankind, something is stirring. Call it instinct, an instinct that man has almost destroyed within himself; but it is still there. People *know* that something crucial is happening.

One of the first manifestations of the new consciousness was the emergence of the 'flower children' of the 1960's Young people began to rebel not just against the establishment but against the whole attitude of the previous generation. And what started then, although decried by older people who realised that their entire way of life and thinking was being challenged, has since spread like wildfire. Now, huge sections of western society are not only aware of the planetary crisis but are actively doing something about it in whatever way they can. Indeed, a great number of spirits have recently chosen to incarnate for the specific purpose of dealing with this unique turning point in the world's history. It is up to you to recognise, help and support these incoming souls.

Following increasing political and social unrest, there will be economic instability. You have already had a foretaste of this. In industry, for example, it is no longer merely a struggle between workers and management. Something far deeper is beginning to manifest. It is the rising up like bile of some of the rottenness that has accrued on this planet; it is the urge to resist that rottenness by raising yourself above it and uplifting others with you.

So, looking ahead, it is going to be a difficult but rewarding period for those who have found the love I have spoken of. We have arrived at a great moment in human history. The moment when supreme love is going to reach out, even into the most stony and unawakened heart in the world.

This is the time to stand up and be counted. You are

aboard a lovely planet that provides anything and everything you need. Why should you allow greed and envy and fear to destroy all that?

Strange as it may seem, the future of this planet is not pre-determined; in fact you are creating that future all the time by your every thought, action and deed, and this is why the spreading of light is so important. One does not have to convert or force anyone. Every single person can play a vital part for, if you meditate and send out light every day, then you are making a significant contribution to the future: you are affecting the future. *You are the future*. All those incarnate at this time are truly privileged for this is one of the most interesting periods in the history and evolution of planet Earth and you are part of that history, part of that evolution.

Time is short, for you are caught in this process of acceleration. Yet through your love, through your kindness and dedication, you have to remove the need for that acceler-ation. Not take it away, not stop it, not destroy it, but remove the need for it and gently guide this transformation from adolescent humanity to adult humanity. In piloting spaceship Earth through this stage of your spiritual reawakening, you will learn to find yourselves as individuals, as whole beings.

The angelic forces obviously wish to see mankind rise above the need for catastrophe, to rise above the need for war, torture and suffering. None of these things are God-wished. The sooner mankind can come to that realisation, the safer the planet will become, ecologically and in every way. You have the free will, it is your decision.

Even now, 'ordinary' men and women are beginning to stand up for themselves, to think for themselves, to question policies with which they disagree and by which they for others are offended or betrayed.

Mankind is at last beginning to face its own shadow, the only remedy for transformation, and through that growing awareness and awakening it is becoming more human, more caring.

I have every confidence that, as humanity wakes from its long and troubled sleep, this great work *will* be accomplished.

''Thank you, Michael for your loyalty to Merlin and me. . .

''. . .I thank you all for preserving in this book the essence of love, compassion and forgiveness, for these are the energies now released by the withdrawal of Excalibur.

The sword is now standing over this book; may its light reach into the darkest corners of the planet.''

H-A

Tony Neate was born in Streatham, South London, in October 1929. He has worked as a sensitive for over 30 years and the wisdom from his source, H-A, has provided the philosophy upon which The Atlanteans was founded. Together with his wife and three other families he founded the Runnings Park Conference Centre in West Malverns, Worcestershire

Tony is a healer and a founder/tutor of the College of Healing. He is deeply involved in the field of nutrition and the hostilic approach to the treatment of cancer and is a trustee and Chairman of the management committee of New Approaches to Cancer. Tony is a council member of the College of Psychic Studies and, since the retirement of Sir George Trevelyan, is Chairman of the Wrekin Trust.

A novelist and screenwriter, Michael Dean was born in London. He worked for Southern Television in 1958, and later ran a studio in London training actors and actresses for the camera. He helped to launch Radio Caroline in 1964 and co-wrote three novels with Robert Donaldson. In recent years he has been introducing a new subject into schools and colleges: 'OURSELVES, the first subject in our education.' In 1966 Michael 'stumbled on' the Ancient Wisdom, which has since taken him on 'a long and inspiring inner journey that never ceases to amaze' him. It is in the re-emergence of this once-hidden knowledge that he believes we shall find the key to our survival.

The dramatic story of the entrance of H-A
into the lives of Tony Neate and his
companions, and of the growth of the
Atlanteans and of their eventual arrival at
Runnings Park in the Malvern Hills, is told
by Annie Wilson in *Where There's Love*,
published by Gateway Books, 19 Circus
Place, Bath BA1 2PW, (192 pp, UK price
£3.95, US price $6.95)

If you want to know more about the
Atlanteans, please contact them at:
Runnings Park, Croft Bank, West Malvern,
Worcs, WR14 4BP.